Plenty Good Room

Plenty Good Room

WOMEN VERSUS MALE POWER IN THE BLACK CHURCH

Marcia Y. Riggs

The Pilgrim Press · Cleveland

The Pilgrim Press, 700 Prospect Avenue, Cleveland, Ohio
44115-1100
pilgrimpress.com
© 2003 Marcia Y. Riggs

With Scenarios written by the Rev. Joan C. Speaks.
Reprinted by permission.

From *Race Rules: Navigating the Color Line* by Michael
Eric Dyson, copyright © 1996 by Michael Eric Dyson.
Reprinted by permission of Perseus Books Publishers,
a member of Perseus Books, L.L.C.

From *Illuminata* by Marianne Williamson, copyright
© 1994 by Marianne Williamson. Used by permission
of Random House, Inc.

Printed in the United States of America on acid-free paper

08   07   06   05   04   03   5   4   3   2   1

Library of Congress Cataloguing-in-Publication Data

Riggs, Marcia.
    Plenty good room : women versus male power in the
Black church / Marcia Y. Riggs.
        p.   cm.
    Includes bibliographical references (p.) and index.
    ISBN 0-8298-1508-2
    1. African American churches.   2. Sex role—Religious
aspects—Christianity.   3. Womanist theology.   4. Sexual
ethics.   I. Title.

BR563.N4R53   2002
277.3'083'08996073—dc21

                                        2002193052

TO MY SISTERS AND BROTHERS,

Helen L. Allen,
Claudesta L. Riggs,
Stephen F. Riggs,
S. Kevin Riggs, Sr.

and

All the sisters and brothers
in the church who seek
understanding about how
to be sisters and brothers
in Christ

C O N T E N T S

PREFACE 9

ACKNOWLEDGMENTS 15

ONE / Introduction 17

TWO / Shaking the Foundation 31
*An Interpretation of African American
Sexual Gender Relations*

THREE / Standing in yet outside the Gates 65
*The African American Church
as a Site of Sexual Gender Oppression*

FOUR / Our Hope Is Built on . . . 93
*Rudiments for Transforming the Moral Life
of the African American Church*

POSTSCRIPT 121

ENDNOTES 127

BIBLIOGRAPHY 137

INDEX 149

PREFACE

The subject matter found in this book was originally presented as lectures and workshops under the title, "Asking Unspeakable Questions: Transforming the Moral Life of the African American Church." There were two primary reasons for that title. First, every time I presented a lecture on the subject of this book, African American church folks have been disturbed that I would expose the black church in this way—that I would "air our dirty linen" in public. Second, this book examines the subject of sexual-gender ethics,[1] and it is again my experience that the subject of sex and the African American church (as is the case with most other churches also) remains a largely taboo subject, calling for discretion if not downright secrecy (unless we're condemning the sexual promiscuity of teenagers or the sexual "immorality" of homosexual persons). Thus, I was asking unspeakable questions in the sense that I dared to question taken-for-granted assumptions and practices of our life together in the African American church. Indeed, the matters under discussion in this book are difficult ones because I criticize the African American church, the church that has been on the forefront of struggles for justice in society. How dare I?

I dare to do so for two reasons. First, sexual-gender relations in the churches have reached a critical moment. Recent events in one denomination are illustrative. In December 1999 a female minister won a sexual harassment case against the African Methodist Episcopal Church in Kansas City.[2] In August 2000 that same denomination elected its first female bishop—an accomplishment that "required more than a century of struggle to accomplish."[3] To me, these two events point to the problematic character of sexual-gender relations in the churches. The African American church can be a place where women are subject to sexual harassment for which they must seek redress through channels outside the church, and the church can be a place where women's challenges to its institutional sexism lead to gender-based tokenism rather than value-based institutional changes that would undergird a truly gender-inclusive church. I realize that this position may seem to belittle the accomplishments of individual women as well as the history of women's leadership in African American churches; I do not intend to do that. Instead, my analysis focuses on the experience of women and men as gender social groups in the church as a social institution.

Second, I dare to offer this analysis because this is the church of my faith development and nurture. This is the place where I came to believe in the God of justice and love, and it is also the place where I have come to know exclusion because I am a woman who doesn't want to go along with the way that things have always been. Thus, I offer this book as an outgrowth of my faith journey in the African American church and as an ethicist who is deeply concerned about the distorted relationship between the professed theological and ethical beliefs and moral practices with respect to gender in that church. In particular, I am concerned with the way that we reinterpret our beliefs about justice in order to match our sexual-gender oppressive practices while maintaining that we "received" such interpretation by way of the Bible and/or church tradition.

In this book I offer both descriptive analysis and normative proposals for transforming the moral life of the African American church in the areas of sexual-gender relations, clergy ethics, ministerial ethics, and ecclesial practices. The African American church is a case study for this analysis and these proposals because I am doing womanist liberation Christian ethical reflection. Generally, Christian ethical reflection is analysis of the morality (virtues, values, ideals, duties, responsibilities) practiced by persons and communities of faith who profess belief in Jesus Christ. Such analysis means that we examine the sources of our morality—the Bible, doctrine, theology, and experience of the faithful throughout the ages. We examine these sources both with appreciation and criticism as the sources also critique us. Doing womanist[4] Christian ethical reflection means

that authentic ethical reflection begins with the particular experiences of African American women in the various dimensions of their lived experiences—historical,
religious/spiritual, political, familial, woman-centered,
woman-identified—in specific contexts of their lives. In
this book, this means that I am using African American
women's experience as the lens through which the
African American church's moral understanding of gender is assessed both appreciatively and critically. In this
case, it also means that I acknowledge straightforwardly
the perspective from which I do my ethical analysis—as
an African American Christian woman who was bap-
tized, ordained, and has practiced ministry in a historical African American denomination. It is liberation
Christian ethical reflection because it affirms that societal or institutional morality can conceal oppressive relations, and unveiling those relationships is an appropriate point of departure for doing ethical reflection. In
this book, unveiling relationships of gender oppression
in the African American church is the point of departure for this analysis.

I offer scenarios throughout the text to introduce
and illustrate issues being analyzed. These scenarios
represent composite real, lived experiences of individuals as those experiences shed light on our common life
in the church. I feel confident speaking of the composite scenarios as representative of experiences common
to life in the church because the writer of the scenarios
(except for one that is excerpted from another published work), the Rev. Joan C. Speaks, has been a pastor, teacher, and counselor to ministers in training and
full-fledged ministers in the African American churches

for over twenty years. Also, when I have used these scenarios in lectures and workshops, persons have told me how much their experiences resonated with them.

The first chapter of the book gives definitions and outlines the theories used to do the analysis throughout the book. Chapters 2 and 3 analyze sexual-gender relations with respect to ethical dimensions of sexual-gender injustice that arises in these areas: (1) laywomen and male clergy; (2) gender and the call; (3) preaching and sexuality; (4) homosexuality and ministry; (5) men, women, and leadership. At the beginning of each chapter, there are scenarios, and I ask questions for further reflection on the scenario and what will be discussed in the chapter. At the end of chapters 2–4, I propose an exercise for dialogue; these questions and exercises are tools to be used in transforming the moral life of the church. In the concluding chapter, chapter 4, I present rudiments of sexual-gender ethics, clergy ethics, and ministerial ethics for the African American church that has sexual-gender justice as central to its identity and practices. In a postscript I suggest the implications of this analysis of the African American church for doing ethical reflection on sexual-gender ethics and clergy ethics in other church contexts.

ACKNOWLEDGMENTS

My special thanks to Columbia Theological Seminary for a sabbatical leave that was granted to me during my receipt of a post-doctoral fellowship from the Womanist Consortium of the University of Georgia, Athens. It was during that leave and with the support of the women of the Consortium that I was able to conceive the ideas and begin writing this book. I am also grateful for feedback that I received when I offered versions of the ideas contained in this book as lectures for the African American Experience in Theological Education Lectures at Memphis Theological Seminary and as a presenter on a panel of the Society of Christian Ethics and the Womanist Approaches to Religion and Society Group of the American Academy of Religion. Special thanks to Joanne

DeMark for coaching me through a serious writing block and Kim Sadler at The Pilgrim Press for support as well as patience.

This book has taken longer than I anticipated to complete, but I thank God for renewal of my health and the capacity for analysis and creativity so that this book can now bear fruit.

1

INTRODUCTION

Before getting to the heart of this ethical analysis, it is important to clarify the way that I am using terms and the theory that drives the analysis. First, what do I mean by the black or African American church? I am using the term black or African American church to refer to those congregational settings where African American Christians predominate: congregants and leaders of independent, historically black-controlled denominations and members and leaders in local congregations within white mainline denominations.[1] I realize that the use of the term black or African American church seems to ignore the pluralism that characterizes African American religious experience and churches. However, I join established scholarship in using the term black or African American church "as a

17

kind of sociological and theological shorthand reference to the pluralism of black Christian churches in the
United States."[2] Also, although I will use the terms
black and African American interchangeably, most
often I will use the term African American so as to
bring to mind the idea that African psychological, cultural, and ethical residuals in the collective consciousness of black people in the United States are part of a
creative and conflictual source of the identity and behavior of black people because of the history of slavery
and white racism. This definition of the term is important because this ethical analysis is focused upon intragroup dynamics—what I refer to as the internal dimension of black oppression.[3] In other words, this ethical
analysis is concerned with the moral life that African
Americans create within the churches where they are in
control of the leadership and constitute the majority of
the membership. This does not mean that I ignore the
context of white racist oppression in which this moral
life is enacted, but that larger context is not the point
of departure for this analysis. Rather, it is the moral
subjectivity and agency of African Americans themselves that is primary here, and the larger context is examined insofar as it contributes to and constrains the
way that African Americans create, express, and maintain their moral life. The overarching ethical framework
evaluates where African American women and men are
along this moral agency axis—complicity $\leftrightarrow$ accountability $\leftrightarrow$ responsibility—with regard to sexual-gender
relations within the African American church. What are
dynamics of male-female relations that denote complicity in sexual-gender oppression? How do men and

women become accountable—become aware of those dynamics and seek consciously to break their complicity with such? What are the earmarks of responsible, liberating sexual-gender relations?

Furthermore, the African American church is being examined as "a supportive institution" of society and as "a human community."[4] In a conflict model of society, there is reciprocal interaction between determinative institutions (political and economic) and supportive institutions (law, education, religion, media, family), and there is a social morality that those institutions either reinforce or challenge. To speak of the church as a human community is to offer a social interpretation that acknowledges that the church is a community ("a body of persons who share some measure of common life, and a common loyalty") that fulfills the following functions:

(1) a natural community—it addresses physical and social needs of human beings;

(2) a political community—it establishes an order to execute its purpose;

(3) a community of language—its members communicate using a common language that distinguishes them from those outside the community;

(4) a community of interpretation—it provides specific meanings of key terms and symbols that constitutes the distinctive beliefs and the identity of the community;

(5) a community of memory and understanding—it retains its identity over time because its members share a common memory of important events that are retold and relived; and

(6) a community of belief and action—its members share a commitment and a professed loyalty that is expressed through actions.

This analysis explicates the way that the African American church in its function as a supportive institution in U.S. society tends to reinforce (mostly unintentionally) rather than challenge the racist, patriarchal, capitalist social morality that supports sexual-gender oppression, and how being a human community of sexual-gender beings impacts the African American church's self-understanding and practices within its own walls and in society. As a supportive social institution and human community, into what sexual-gender morality does the African American church socialize its members?

Second, why do I speak of the *moral life* of the African American church? I have chosen to use the term moral life because I intend to examine both the character (the being) and the agency (the doing) of these churches. By character, I mean the virtues, values, and ideals that characterize the dispositions of individuals and the ends toward which the church strives. By agency, I am referring both to the formal and informal practices of the churches. Some important features of practices are:

(1) They are indispensable to moral formation.

(2) They are those particularly pregnant actions that are both a means to a good life and are also aspects of a historically constituted good form of life.

(3) They are those actions intrinsic to a way of life that center, sustain, and order that way of living.

(4) They are rites that embody what is right.[5]

The practices of churches are formal when they are mandated by the doctrines and polity of the churches; in this analysis, the sacraments, such as baptism and the eucharist, are such practices. Practices are informal when they may or may not be spoken or written into official documents of the church, but they are consistently adhered to as a normative way to order the life of the church. Depending on the denominational affiliation of a church, the placing of doilies on the heads of women receiving communion may be a formal or an informal practice. Both the character and agency of the church derive from a moral vision that provides a structure of meaning that signifies what is perceived and affirmed as good and evil, acceptable and unacceptable, responsible and irresponsible. What virtues, values, or ideals characterize moral life that nurtures liberating sexual-gender relations? How do practices (formal and informal) reinforce and support oppressive sexual-gender relations, and how might these practices be transformed? What moral vision is needed to support transformed sexual-gender relations?

Third, to what does *sexual-gender ethics* refer? Sexual-gender ethics refers to the morality governing the relations between women and men who are biologically different beings (sexual) with socially constructed meanings of being female and male (gender) that they bring to both their private and public interactions. This analysis of sexual-gender ethics is premised upon the following definition of oppression and uses practice-based power and gender theory as well as social construction of gender theory as a perspective for doing Christian sexual ethics as the framework through which to examine the morality of sexual-gender relations in the African American church.

A WORKING DEFINITION OF *OPPRESSION*

Oppression refers to the processes by which relationships of imbalanced power between social groups are maintained, thus privileging one group over another and thereby limiting, injuring, and or controlling the less privileged group. These processes are "embedded in unquestioned norms, habits, and symbols, in institutional rules and the collective consequences of following those rules."[6]

By using a definition that refers to processes and social groups, I intend to do an analysis that is more concerned with the practices (rather than the origins) of sexual-gender oppression in the African American church and that stresses the importance of the site (for example, home, school, or church) for understanding oppression. This means that I place current practices into sociohistorical and sociopyschological perspective, seeking to disclose the sexual-gender dynamics that constitute these practices; then, I offer a qualitative interpretation of such dynamics and practices. By focusing on African American women and men as social groups, the analysis presupposes this: Individual women and men derive a sexual-gender identity from their gender social group's history and experience that informs their moral agency individually and communally. In the specific context of the African American church, it is critical to come to understand the way that sexual-gender relations "involve a power relationship in which the subjectivity of personal experience is intertwined with the objectivity of collective and political relationships."[7] Importantly, one of the ways that male power is being examined here is in terms of the understanding that power is "a process of human interaction;" "it takes place between interacting members of a relationship."[8] In other words, in the context of the African American church, male power is fostered through the interaction of women and men whose individual sexual identities (personal experiences) are inextricably based in the history and experience of their gender social groups (collective sociohistorical and sociopsychological experiences) in the United States.

PRACTICE-BASED THEORY OF POWER AND GENDER

A practice-based theory of power and gender relations ties together the emphases on practices and power as a process of human interaction:

> In practice-based theory the structure of gender relations is seen as historically composed. Practices create a structure that constrains further practice, although practices may also resist those constraints. Practice-based theory posits that the construction of masculinity is both personal and social, requiring inventive action and reflexive knowledge at the same time that social rules, resources and politics in any practice are engaged.[9]

According to this theory, there are three different but interrelated structures of relationships between men and women throughout history: (1) structure of labor,

(2) structure of power, and (3) structure of desire. The structure of labor refers to the division of labor, that is, the organization and practices of paid/unpaid work, men's and women's jobs, and so on. The structure of power refers to a hierarchy of authority, control, and/or coercion, and "power may be an imbalance of advantage or an inequality of resources." The structure of desire refers to "desirability of an other," that is, homosexual/heterosexual relations, the antagonism of gender, and the like.[10] In this analysis, the contention is that male power is a result of the way that the interrelated structures of labor, power, and desire are distinctively configured and operative in the African American church.

SOCIAL CONSTRUCTION OF GENDER THEORY AND CHRISTIAN ETHICS

- Social scientists distinguish between "sex," which is, in fact, a biologically based category, and "gender," which refers to the particular set of socially constructed meanings that are associated with each sex.

  The interpretation of what it is to be a woman or a man is a socioculturally constructed difference that reflects and perpetuates the prevailing distribution of power and privilege in an institution or society.

- The socioculturally constructed differences between women and men are hierarchically related, such that women are perceived as deficient (inferior) or deviant (evil) from a male-biased norm.

24

- Differences between women and men that are understood as deficiency or deviance from a male-biased norm are used to rationalize sexism.

The decision to use social construction of gender theory as the framework for this analysis aligns with a quest for a Christian postmodern sexual ethic that Christine E. Gudorf outlines. Gudorf suggests that social construction theory offers us in the church a way to hold in tension the desire for order and the search for relationality and justice that individuals and groups dominated by hegemonic sexual norms seek. According to Gudorf, social construction theory offers a way that may help us to accomplish the difficult task of rethinking sexual ethics in the quest for some agreed-upon meanings for sexuality as the church seeks to engage in public discourse.

Importantly, social construction theory is a means for reconstruing traditional sources for ethical thinking in the churches. For example, from a constructionist point of view, the theological basis for a Catholic natural law approach to sexuality that uses biological and social science as methods for "discerning divine intentions within an evolving, dynamic creation" reads thus:

Understanding creation in terms of a process initiated and overseen by God sets the stage for the social construction of sexuality as neither a usurpation of God's right, nor a denial of divine intentions, much less as an irreligious, secular task, but as one aspect of the larger task of Christians to create ourselves and our society in the likeness of the Kingdom of God that Jesus announced.[11]

Likewise, the Methodist "quadrilateral" sources for Christian ethics—scripture, tradition, reason, and experience—do not need to be abandoned when using this theory. A socially constructed Christian sexual ethics understands these sources thus:

> (A) Scripture gives us stories about what kind of persons we should be as well as stories that assure us of God's continuing grace and forgiveness. Scripture is accordingly only indirectly a guide for behavior—sexual or otherwise.
>
> (B) Reason is necessary if experience is to be valuable in the work of ethics.
>
> (C) Experience is a source for discerning God's revelation in scripture and tradition (i.e., creeds, liturgical and ethical practices, histories of Christian communities) that must be interpreted. Reason and the sciences are critical for doing that interpretation.
>
> (D) Tradition is revelatory when it reflects some consensus of the faithful, general compatibility with the rest of Christian tradition proceeding from Jesus Christ, and promotes the common good of the entire community. "Recourse to tradition in the construction of a contemporary Christian sexual ethic requires a constant vigilance in discerning pollutants such as patriarchy, racism, sexism, and bi-sexual dualism from the living water of revelation."[12]

Finally, to socially construct Christian sexual ethics means that we must face our fear in the churches that to do so will lead us to relativize our sexual norms using cultural standards rather than biblical ones. We in the churches are pushed from this theoretical perspective to consider:

(1) Accepting responsibility for constructing a sexual ethic for humans rather than displacing responsibility for human codes onto God.

(2) Recognizing that what Christian faith and tradition contribute to the construction of a sexual ethic is not specific sexual rules, but the concept of behavioral limits based in concern for the dignity and welfare of all persons, for justice between groups, and for love of neighbor and the common good.[13]

A primary mechanism in the social construction of gender is social mythology. Social myths are ideas about social reality that are bound up with emotion and with what we fear may happen and/or what we hope will come true. As ideas that reinforce fear or hope, they oppose belief to fact, thus effectively changing and/or obscuring facts. These ideas describe and prescribe our behavior as we internalize them; they function to inscribe accepted beliefs about social reality and our places in that reality. Also, social myths become part and parcel of interpretation and justification for the way things are, even if the interpretation and justification are illogical. While these ideas may or may not be based upon sacred texts or scientific evidence, the efficacy of the ideas derives from the way they make sense of the world for us.[14]

Those persons in society or an institution (such as the church) with power are those who interpret these ideas (social myths) and influence the behavior of others through that interpretation. Importantly, the power of these persons may be legitimate in that these persons have been elected to a position or are installed in a position by members of the society or institution, but they may come to misuse their power by dominating or manipulating others through actions such as threat of force or force, or interpretations that devalue and demean. One aim of the analysis in this book is to expose the social mythology of African American womanhood and manhood and how that mythology drives sexual-gender relationships in the church and impacts the moral life of the church. What values and ideals accompany the internalization and adaptation of sexual-gender social myths?

Fourth, what is *clergy ethics? Ministerial ethics?* Clergy ethics refers to any formal (usually written) or informal code of conduct prescribed for clergy or others acting in a ministerial role by a denomination and/or the role morality that is practiced by persons who are ordained to fulfill the role of clergy in a church. Ministerial ethics here refers to the values and practices of a church's common life, that is, the ethics of the church's life that enables its ministry within and witness outside its walls. Ministerial ethics is used as an overarching category, allowing examination of the interrelated ethics of clergy and laity sharing a common life and call to ministry. The relationship between clergy and laity is here understood as the heart of the church's ability to do ministry; thus, ministerial ethics might also be thought of as the ethics of the church's common good. Thus, the emphasis of this analysis is twofold: (1) the ethics of the relationship between clergy and laity and (2) the role morality of clergy rather than formulated clergy codes of conduct. Clergy ethics and ministerial ethics might address a variety of areas of professional and personal, sexual and nonsexual conduct, for example, breach of confidentiality, cheating on income taxes, theft. However, I am focusing on the intersection of sexual-gender ethics, clergy ethics, and ministerial ethics because I think that these are critical points of contention within the moral life of the African American church.

In sum, in this book, I am doing social constructionist Christian ethical analysis of sexual/gender relations between African American women and men in the context of the African American church. I am examining the African American church as a site of sexual-gender oppression in which male power (as clergy exercising patriarchal privilege) operates consciously and unconsciously to create sexism and heterosexism, and how such sexual-gender oppression is mediated through ecclesial practices. This analysis is interrogating the interrelationship between the sociohistorical and interpersonal dimensions of sexual-gender oppression in the African American church. In other words, I am exposing the relationship between African American women and men as distinct, yet interrelated sexual-gender groups whose shared history of race, gender, and economic oppression in the United States circumscribes their sexual-gender relations individually and collectively. Lastly, this analysis proceeds from the assumption that intentional human agency is critical to moral and institutional transformation. The book is thus an invitation to members of the African American church to engage intentionally in creating sexual-gender justice in the church and society.

SHAKING THE FOUNDATIONS

An Interpretation
of African American
Sexual-Gender Relations

This is the challenge we face as black men and women in America. Our survival as a race is predicated upon our ability to relate to each other as equals. We must begin by recognizing and honoring our differences as men and women, and devise ways to use our differences and complementary strengths to enrich our visions and our joint struggles. As Paulo Freire admonished, "The true focus of revolutionary change is never merely the oppressive situations that we seek to escape, but that piece of the oppressor that is planted deep within each of us, and that knows only the oppressor's tactics, the oppressor's relationships."

We have arrived where we are today by traveling on a long, hard road, one that was not wholly of our own choosing. The path ahead is long as well, and the way is steep. But if we choose it, and if we learn to walk together as comrades, we will, at long last, lighten the load.

Let the healing begin.[1]

— Donna L. Franklin

What is a Black man in an institutionally racist society, in the social system of modern capitalist America? The essential tragedy of being Black and male is our inability, as men and as people of African descent, to define ourselves without the stereotypes the larger society imposes upon us, and through various institutional means perpetuates and permeates within our entire culture. Our relations with our sisters, our parents and children, and indeed across the entire spectrum of human relations are imprisoned by images of the past, false distortions that seldom if ever capture the essence of our being. We cannot come to terms with Black women until we understand the half-hidden stereotypes that have crippled our development and social consciousness. We cannot challenge racial and sexual inequality, both within the Black community and across the larger American society, unless we comprehend the critical difference between the myths about ourselves and the harsh reality of being Black men.[2]

— Manning Marable

SCENARIO A

Dear Journal:

I look out of the window each time a car passes. Where is he? He promised to be here. Why isn't he? I'm always the one waiting. He tells me to be more patient. He always reminds me that God has called me to this relationship. He tells me that God wants me to be his soul mate and that I should be grateful that God has given me such a role to play in his life. I remember the first time I saw him, standing in the pulpit, with his six-foot frame covered in the most beautiful robe I had ever seen, white with red velvet on the panels and trimmed in gold. Large sleeves made the movement of his arms seem celestial. If not God, definitely Gabriel. You knew just looking at his angelic face, that whatever would come forth had to be a message from on high. His voice transported you to the gates of heaven, a sonorous baritone that demanded ever so gently that you must hear him. I knew immediately that we would have something special. There must be a place for me in his life and work. That was the first Sunday he was with us.

That was more than ten years ago, and I have been right by his side since that first Sunday. It didn't take long for him to see how much he needed me and I needed him. At first it was just work in the office, pick up his robes from the cleaners, and make sure his appointment book was kept well. It progressed to driving him to speaking engagements out of town and producing not only the bulletin for the church but special programs and brochures for the nursery. We worked well together. His thoughts were my thoughts. I knew what he was going to say before he said it. Even though the other sisters in the church were jealous, they commented on how well Rev. and I got things done. Of course, all that working and planning and producing together brought us together as a couple, until Rev. said that we needed to experience the gift that God had given men and women through sexuality. I hadn't planned to go that far. In fact, I really didn't think that he would ask that of me. But when he did I felt chosen of God. This was my pastor, my shepherd, asking me to give something special to him, something that would help him keep going and giving. I felt like Mary must have felt when Gabriel gave her the news. God has called me to do this?! But just like anything God calls you to—it's never easy.

Now we hardly have time to be with each other. So much work has to be done, we rarely have time to be close anymore. He leaves messages on my machine about the work that needs to be done, but he's always running off to some meeting. Sister Coward says Rev. is spending more and more time with Sister Saint. I know that she is trying to say something about their relationship, but I'm not going to listen. The sisters are always talking about Rev. and someone in the congregation.

Last week when he didn't keep our date I confronted him at the office about he and Sister Saint. He was shocked that I would even think something like that. He accused me of being like the other old women in the church. I was just angry; I shouldn't have done that. He has been so good to me. I asked the Lord to forgive me for my anger and my thoughts. I went back to Rev. the next day, and he was willing to forgive me for my indiscretion. It really has been wonderful taking care of him so that he can take care of the church.

Another hour, ten more cars, and no Rev. Those deacons need to let that man have some peace. I think I'll make Rev. something special; I know he'll be here soon.

Questions for reflection:

> What are the dynamics of oppressive sexual-gender relations between African American women and men that undergird the situation described in this scenario?

> What virtues and values might guide the moral agency of African American women and men who are seeking to break complicity with these dynamics?

> What happens to these relationships in the context of the church?

There are a number of issues pertinent to the subject of sexual-gender relations between African American women and men and their life in the church in this scenario that opens the chapter. However, the focus of this chapter is the sexual-gender relations that have developed as African American women and men relate to one another in terms of a sexual-gender morality that reflects psychological adaptation of normative sociocultural sexual-gender social myths rather than from norms that they might construct in light of historical and cultural particularities of being African American women and men. This chapter will propose an answer to the question: What are the dynamics of oppressive sexual-gender relations between African American women and men that undergird the situation described in this scenario?

In her book, *What's Love Got To Do with it?: Understanding and Healing the Rift between Black Men and Women,* sociologist Donna L. Franklin locates the origins of black gender conflict in "the experience of powerlessness" during slavery. Specifically, slaveholders had "absolute control over the intimate lives of the slaves"; they controlled the slave's selection of a marital partner, decided how long couples could stay together, and forced separation of families. The exercise of this absolute control resulted in the "dismantling of black manhood and womanhood" as neither men or women were able to fulfill their gender roles in ways normative to their West African background. Men who would have matured into husbands, fathers, and/or warriors were denied the rites of passage by which they would have achieved those roles in their African context. Likewise, women who would have become cherished wives and mothers had these roles dishonored as they were raped and their children became the legal property of the slaveholder. As enslaved men and women survived such humiliation and brutality, "the roots of black gender conflict" were laid.[3] Franklin summarizes these roots in this way:

> The black male was marginalized from the family because planters and slave traders frequently perceived the black family as consisting of just

the slave mother and her children. As sales were negotiated, husbands and fathers were often not included as part of the deal but were "un-bundled"—like a commodity—from the family unit. Not only did wives lose husbands but husbands lost wives and their children. The forced (or threatened) dissolution of not only marital but familial relationships meant that slaves could not develop the interdependency that characterized most marital relationships; they could be separated and sold away from each other at any time.

Moreover, slave wives could not rely on their husbands for the care and protection that was almost universally expected of men at the time; nor could slave men provide for them. This was likely the most frustrating aspect of slavery's effects on gender relations, and it laid the foundation for the anger and distrust that persist between black men and women to this day.[4]

With emancipation, freed men and women sought to legalize their marriages and establish family life on their own terms, especially the decision that women would no longer work in the fields in order to care for their families at home. However, their efforts were complicated by external economic pressures. The Freedman's Bureau established by the government in 1865 played a critical role in exerting external economic pressure. One of the roles of the Bureau was to monitor labor contracts between freed slaves and planters under the sharecropping system. As planters complained to the Bureau about the reduction of the black labor force because women (especially mothers) were not working in the fields, the Bureau mandated the return of the women to the fields. The Bureau enforced this mandate by enabling men to sign contracts for the labor of their entire families, paying women lower wages for the same labor, and allotting less land to families without a male head of house. In effect, "The Faustian bargain struck by white and black men —designating the black man as head of household, allocating him higher wages, and giving him authority over black women in exchange for their labor in the fields—was the first signal after emancipation of the erosion of gender relations in the African American community."[5]

From the slavery era through emancipation, African American women and men found themselves bound together under racist-capitalist-patriarchal oppression. However, the consequences of that shared oppression were different for the two gender social groups. African American women were characterized as a subspecies of women; their womanhood was assessed by the ideals of a nineteenth-century ideology of true womanhood that purported the virtues of women were submissiveness, domesticity, piety, and purity. Bond and free women— field workers, domestics, professionals—were a gender social group subjected to sexual assaults and economic exploitation through a perverse logic deriving from the ideology of true womanhood. This perverse logic asserted that all African American women were rendered immoral because of the race's history of slavery. Womanhood was defined by a white racist, patriarchal socioethical norm that idealized white women and debased black women.

According to a white racist, patriarchal norm for manhood, African American men were inferior. Indeed, the nineteenth-century ideology of the Negro child/savage characterized them as needing the guidance and control of superior white men. Bond and free African American men were a gender social group subjected to degradation of their manhood and economic exploitation because they could not function in the roles of provider and protector ascribed to men by a white racist, patriarchal socioethical norm for manhood. This norm deified white men and emasculated black men.

The following racial sexual-gender social mythology of the four gender social groups—white men, white women, black men, black women—summarizes the nineteenth-century social construction of gender:

> White men are omnipotent, providers, and protectors.
>
> White women are impotent, frivolous, and vulnerable.
>
> Black men are powerless, spineless, and unreliable.
>
> Black women are strong, physically invulnerable, and emotionally callous.[6]

From the perspective of this racial-sexual social mythology, the power of white men derives from their place at the top of the hierarchy, thus constituting them as the normative standard not only for manhood, but for humanity—both male and female. Consequently, the subordination of white women consists in portraying them as in need of the power, benevolence, and protection of white men. The subordination of black men is established by labeling them as the antithesis of white men; they are the inverse of a man (per the standard for white manhood)—an inferior man without masculine virtues. The subordination of black women derives from the denial that they possessed the character of womanhood (per the standard for white womanhood) and the attribution of character traits that make them more masculine than black men. This social mythology reminds us that the social construction of manhood and womanhood depends on a hierarchy of relations that manifests a balancing of extremes and antitheses between gender groups, and that hierarchical relationships are power relationships (one group is privileged in relation to another group).

The perduring effects of this racial-sexual social mythology since emancipation through today are cultural as well as political, intercommunal as well as intracommunal, individual as well as collective. Stereotypes of African American women and men found in contemporary media portrayals and public policy proposals are based in this mythology. Jezebel, Sapphire, Mammy, Aunt Jemima, Welfare Queen, Sambo, Bigger Thomas, Jack Johnson, and Uncle Tom—such are the stereotypes framing the lives of and responses to African American women and men, respectively. These stereotypes undergird the way the dominant culture perceives and responds to African American women and men as well as the way these women and men characterize and respond to one another today.

A landmark contemporary example of the interrelationship between sexual-gender social mythology and its significance to public perception and policy discussion affecting the lives of black women and men based upon their gender relations was the 1965 Moynihan Report. The report declared the black family matriarchal and that black women suffered less from racism than black men because they could often find work when black men could not. The author of the report, Daniel Moynihan (a white man who was assistant secretary of labor and director of the Office of Policy Planning and Research in the Johnson administration), maintained that the root of the black community's problems, its matriarchal family, could be addressed by restoring male authority in the home and workplace. "The thinking seemed to be: Just make Black men the lords of their own castles and everything will be all right."[7]

The importance of the Moynihan Report to the analysis here is that it makes evident the way that social mythology can describe and prescribe reality. From the Report's description, it was prescribed that in order for African Americans to flourish in U.S. society, their familial structures and gender relations should conform to dominant white sociocultural, socioethical norms for such. According to this prescription, the survival of the "Race" was contingent upon a stable African American patriarchy in which women were dominated by men.

As men marched with placards proclaiming, "I am a man," the latter days of the civil rights movement earmarked the embrace of this prescription within the African American community. As bell hooks points out:

Once [the civil rights] struggle was perceived as won (i.e., that black people had gained equal rights) then one assertion of our new freedom was to make mainstream socialization about gender roles the norm in black life. In the age of integration, black men asserted masculinist subjectivity not by vigilantly challenging white supremacy but by first insisting on the subordination of women, particularly black women. Suddenly, black men who would never have access to jobs within this capitalist framework that would allow them to provide for families could still feel themselves to be "men." Manhood had been redefined. Manhood was not providing and protecting; it was proved by one's capacity to coerce, control, dominate.

This contemporary shift, more than any other, created a crisis in black life that remains unresolved.[8]

These stereotypes and their sociopolitical impact signify that the end result of the racist-sexist-capitalist oppression of African American women and men is objectification. Cornel West summarizes this process of objectification with respect to black sexuality thus:

Americans are obsessed with sex and fearful of black sexuality. The obsession has to do with a search for stimulation and meaning in a fast-paced, market-driven culture; the fear is rooted in visceral feelings about black bodies fueled by sexual myths of black women and men. The dominant myths draw black women and men ei-

42

ther as threatening creatures who have the potential for sexual power over whites, or as harmless, desexed underlings of a white culture. There is Jezebel (the seductive temptress), Sapphire (the evil, manipulative bitch), or Aunt Jemima (the sexless, long-suffering nurturer). There is Bigger Thomas (the mad and mean predatory craver of white women), Jack Johnson, the super performer—be it in athletics, entertainment or sex—who excels others naturally and prefers women of a lighter hue), or Uncle Tom (the spineless, sexless—or is it impotent?—sidekick of whites). The myths offer distorted, dehumanized creatures whose bodies—color of skin, shape of nose and lips, type of hair, size of hips—are already distinguished from the white norm of beauty and whose feared sexual activities are deemed disgusting, dirty, or funky and considered less acceptable.[9]

Alongside this process of objectification, the internalization of their respective sexual-gender myths by African American women and men has led them to blame themselves and counter-blame one another for the strained, and often hostile, relationships between them. African American women either blame men for not fulfilling their role as providers and protectors or they blame themselves for not being supportive enough of black men, thus denying the sexism of black men and their own vulnerability to sexual harassment and exploitation to which all women in a patriarchal society are subject. African American men either blame women for not being feminine enough and disrespectful of black men or they blame themselves for failing to provide security (financial or otherwise) for the women in their lives and become abusive to women and/or homicidal in the black community, thus denying the terror that white racist-sexist-capitalism imposes on the lives of all African American women, men, and children.

In *Stolen Women: Reclaiming Our Sexuality, Taking Back Our Lives*, Gail Elizabeth Wyatt (an African American professor of psychiatry and biobehavioral science) has documented the internalization process through surveys, interviews, and clinical practice with African American women. Wyatt completes her study because she affirms this:

> To the degree that we [African American women] allow our sexual self-image to be defined by others, we will remain as our ancestors were, stolen women, captives, not of strangers but of the past, and of our own unexamined experiences.[10]

To assist African American women in freeing themselves from captivity to the past and destructive sexual self-images, Wyatt reminds them that the forced immigration of African women to the New World sabotaged the meaning of sex (an essential and sacred part of life's plan) and cultural practices (educational or physical rites of passage performed by elder women). She maintains that there are six ways during slavery in which this sabotage occurred:

(1) Sex became a negative experience. The first sexual experience was likely to be rape.

(2) Privacy and modesty were not respected. Women's bodies were exposed and their private parts publicly examined on the auction block.

(3) Group solidarity was difficult to maintain. The African worldview that held that group membership defined and nurtured personal identity was diminished through tactics that divided women using their reproductive capacities as breeders, e.g., women who were house slaves vs. field workers.

(4) Women were often unprepared for their roles. Although women found ways to pass on knowledge important to women's survival from their sexual exploitation (e.g., what herbs to ingest in order to prevent or abort a pregnancy), the African rites of passage could not be practiced as they would have been in their homeland.

(5) Sexual contact between family members was inevitable. The selling of family members at an early age could eventuate in their reunion at such a later time that they did not know one another.

(6) Marriage was no longer protected by the family. The slave owner had final control over marriages.[11]

Under the conditions of slavery, women survived assault upon their sexual selves through psychological adaptation. The first adaptive behavior was to learn to behave one way even if you felt another. The second was not to discuss the kind of abuse that you were experiencing. Silence and secrecy were necessary to survival. The last was that you had to live with a sense of dignity in spite of the abuse.[12] Consequently, stereotypical personality styles have emerged: the Mammy, the She-Devil, and the Workhorse. The Mammy (obese, domesticated, asexual) is the "selfless care giver"; she places others before herself and uses weight to mask her sexuality. The woman living out this personality style is possibly coping with the stress of poverty or feeling unloved through an unhealthy lifestyle (for example, overeating). The She-Devil (immoral, conniving, seductress) is considered basically evil; she is the hypersexual woman who uses her gender and sex as a tool to get what she desires. This woman prefers being seen in a sexual light rather than not being seen at all; in a sense, being sexy is empowering for her. The Workhorse (strong, hard working) values performance and achievement; she may defer her sexual needs and has a very limited notion of what sex should be like. This woman could be a girl gangsta or a well-dressed business executive who is seeking not to feel vulnerable and powerless; in the process, though, this woman actually sacrifices her sexuality so as to be considered respectable in the eyes of the people who matter to her.[13]

Using a questionnaire composed of fourteen statements based upon these stereotypical personality styles, Wyatt surveyed African American women born before World War II or since the 1960s at various educational and economic levels. Eighty-five percent of the women (regardless of age, education, or economic status) endorsed the statements as characteristic of black women.[14] Finally, the messages that women are taught by parents, friends, movies, schools, and the church complete the internalization process. The most clear messages from parents, schools, and the church are about sexual practices that are considered taboo or sinful: nudity, masturbation, premarital intercourse, and homosexuality. Women are warned about sexual abuse as something harmful and to be avoided, but they are not taught what sexual abuse actually is or that it may be perpetrated by family or acquaintances.[15]

How might the character and agency of the laywoman in Scenario A be assessed when we view her through the lens of the stereotypical personality styles? From what is said in the scenario, we find a woman who exhibits attributes of a selfless caregiver and a hard worker as she takes care of the pastor's professional and personal needs, and by extension the needs of the church. Also, because she writes at the beginning of her journal entry, "There must be a place for me in his life and work," we wonder to what extent she may have secured her role in the pastor's life in some manipulative way. Thus, the laywoman is a paradoxical mixture of all three personality styles, as is the case with most women. On one hand, this laywoman is caring and responsible; on the other, she is gullible and irresponsible. Consequently, rather than participating in the life of the church as a woman whose character and agency is grounded in virtues and values such as courage, interdependence, and responsibility, this laywoman becomes complicit in gender injustice as she engages in a relationship with the pastor that diminishes her capacities for self-actualization as well as partnership with men.

In a volume entitled *The American Black Male: His Present Status and His Future,* scholars from a number of academic disciplines analyze black men's lives in the United States. A couple of essays in this volume by Clyde W. Franklin II will be used to explicate black men's internalization of their sexual-gender myths. In the first essay, "Men's Studies, the Men's Movement, and the Study of Black Masculinities: Further Demystification of Masculinities in America," Franklin provides a typology of black masculinities. The founding assumption for Franklin's discussion is this:

> For a variety of reasons, basic tenets of what would become known as "American masculinity" evolved beyond the grasp of Black men. . . . This is not difficult to understand because the model of masculinity in America had been constructed by the patriarchal slave-master system. Clearly, the denial of Black male leadership in America had been promoted, if not dictated, through various and sundry means. . . . As long as the Black male was a slave, property, a thing, he had no claims to being a man. In freedom, however, he was suddenly a human . . . maybe, even a man? But . . . a man provides . . . as the master did, a man is strong . . . as the master was, a man protects . . . as the master did, . . . a man is . . . well . . . a man. He is not a Negro . . . he is a man! By this time the Black male is

begrudgingly recognized as a Negro, but it is questionable whether he is recognized as a man.[16]

The impact of this failure to be recognized as a man has not been accepted passively by black men. There are black men who, in spite of society's failure to recognize them as men, have provided significant public leadership toward black self-determination in the past and present (examples include Frederick Douglass, Booker T. Washington, W. E. B. DuBois, Henry McNeal Turner, Andrew Young, Jesse Jackson, Martin Luther King Jr.). However, such men are considered anomalies or exceptional because they do not fit the dominant society's conception of a black man as defined by sexual-gender myths typified by the stereotypes of Bigger Thomas, Jack Johnson, or Uncle Tom. The internalization process for black men is thus based in a history of not being recognized as men, public leadership on behalf of the race that brands them as anomalies, and sexual-gender social myths that characterize them as "fearsome, threatening, unemployed, irresponsible, potentially dangerous, and generally socially pathological."[17]

Franklin discusses the construction of three black masculinities and a socialization process for black men, which offer important insights into the way that black men come to internalize their sexual-gender social myths. These masculinities and socialization process have three sources: (1) the peer group (usually an age-related cohort), (2) the primary group (two parents or a single parent and siblings or extended family with several generations living together), and (3) mainstream society. Franklin designates these three sources a "lethal socialization triangle" because it produces "types of selves that make Black males enigmas in American society."[18]

"Black male peer group-controlled masculinity" represents attempts by black men to be innovative, seeking to create an identity that is in tension with mainstream society. This masculinity tends to encourage "traits of aggressiveness, violence, competitiveness, heterosexuality, cool poses, dominance, sexism, and passivity/indifference in mainstream society." "Black male primary group-controlled masculinity" derives from the teaching of beliefs and values such as freedom, democracy, individualism, equality of opportunity, the work ethic, and similar values by the primary group. As a result of primary group socialization, male behavior tends to conform to mainstream society's norms and values, and the men are taught survival skills that enable them to distinguish between the ideal and the real when it comes to how black men (as opposed to white men) experience such norms and values. "Mainstream society-controlled black masculinity" is a product of media images of black males that link them to social pathologies in juxtaposition to mainstream society's definition of masculinity, that is, that they assume aggressive, competitive, dominant, and powerful roles in society's basic institutions (the family, the economy, politics, religion, and education). When socialization into this masculinity occurs, black male identity is contradictory and conflictual.[19]

In the second essay, "Ain't I a Man? The Efficacy of Black Masculinities for Men's Studies in the 1990s,"

Franklin stresses the social construction of the black male sex role based in the definition of black male slaves as "subhuman non-men." Given this definition as the point from which black males construct their sex role identity, it is critical to remember that black masculinities are negotiated from "positions of powerlessness" vis a vis powerful white males.[20] Franklin thus characterizes the black male strategies of psychological adaptation using the following fivefold typology of black masculinities that further nuances the earlier threefold one:

Conforming Black masculinity—accepts mainstream society's prescriptions and proscriptions for heterosexual males

Ritualistic Black masculinity—realizes that American societal goals and their individual goals are not coterminous; gradually develop cynical attitudes about individual success and realizing the American dream; appear to be conforming but are ritualistic in their actions, following social dictates

Innovative Black masculinity—responds to blocked opportunities for success in white society in ways that exaggerate an aspect of the dominant masculinity (such as violence) or attain the benefits of such through socially unacceptable means (e.g., drug dealing)

Retreatist Black masculinity—withdraws from American society; have opted out or been forced out of the system; lives characterized by jobless-

ness, welfare dependency, drug addiction, alco-
holism, and homelessness

Rebellious Black masculinity—rejects dominant
society's goals and means of achieving those
goals and constructs ones more compatible
with the interests and welfare of black men.[21]

How do we assess the character and agency of the
pastor in Scenario A in light of these typologies of black
masculinity? As was the case when analyzing the laywoman, the pastor is not easily defined by one of the
types. There is a sense in which the pastor's behavior betrays a contradictory and conflictual black male identity
associated with mainstream-controlled masculinity or
conforming black masculinity. He treats the laywoman in
a manner consistent with dominant society's patriarchal
norms; he exploits her talents, makes her a sexual object,
and is dismissive when challenged by her. However, because his behavior is being acted out in the context of
the African American church, he can be described as operating from a peer group-controlled masculinity or innovative masculinity that reflects an understanding of
clerical status as bestowing patriarchal privilege. In the
context of the church, the pastor affirms his manhood
because he is no longer negotiating his identity in a context of powerlessness and he uses norms of his peer
group (black male clergy) to guide his behavior. (More
will be said about this in the next chapter.) He does not,
therefore, act from a rebellious black masculinity because
his behavior is a kind of black adaptation of dominant
society's norms rather than a break with such.

Living between the objectification of African American sexuality and the internalization of sexual-gender myths about African American women and men, individual African American women and men become caught between personal fulfillment and communal issues. For example, women are labeled antimen and antifamily if they choose lifestyles that do not include marriage and children; men are considered less than men if they do not exhibit sexual prowess, thus they often do so by siring children with a number of women. Apparently caught in reactive postures stemming from the psychological adaptation of dominant culturally based sexual-gender social myths, African American women and men tend to fulfill unspoken, coercive expectations in their sexual-gender relations. Both women and men thus act daily in complicity with sexual-gender oppression.

When African American women and men continue to relate to one another in complicity with sexual-gender oppression, they inscribe this sexual-gender role morality for their sexual- gender social groups respectively:

- Women are to enact the roles of motherhood, either biologically or socially. A "good" black woman supports black men, cares for the black family (and the race), and defends black culture.

- Men are to enact the roles of fatherhood, both biologically and socially. A "good" black man provides for the black family, protects black women, and defines black culture (and the agenda of the race).

In sum, the sexual-gender relations of African American women and men are mostly reactive rather than creative responses to racist-sexist-capitalist oppression under which they both labor. Indeed, their sexual-gender relations are "a kind of social reproductive shadow work"[22] that sustains white racist-sexist-capitalist patriarchal norms for womanhood and manhood. By describing African American sexual-gender relations as social reproductive shadow work, I am suggesting that, when African American women and men live captive to white racist-patriarchal-capitalist norms for manhood and womanhood, their sexual-gender relations sustain white racist-patriarchal-capitalist oppression as well as perpetuate sexual-gender oppression within the African American community.

A significant, public example of how African American sexual-gender relations can do the social reproductive work of sustaining white racist-patriarchal-capitalism while perpetuating sexual-gender oppressive ideas within the African American community is the case of Anita Hill and Clarence Thomas. In 1991 Clarence Thomas, a federal appeals court judge, began the confirmation process to be appointed an associate justice of the Supreme Court. During the confirmation process, Anita Hill, professor of law at the University of Oklahoma, alleged sexual harassment by Judge Thomas in testimony given before the Senate Judiciary Committee. The allegations stemmed from the time when Professor Hill worked under the supervision of Judge Thomas first at the Department of Education (Thomas was an assistant secretary in the Office of Civil Rights) and later at the Equal Employment Opportunity Commission (EEOC).

In her statement, Professor Hill described her experience of sexual harassment as consisting in being repeatedly asked out (after she declined) and graphic talk about sexual matters (pornographic materials and his own sexual prowess). Hill stated that she decided to testify after being asked to do so by the Senate Committee and that she only sought to provide relevant information, having no personal vendetta against the judge. The conclusion to her statement reads as follows:

> I may have used poor judgment early on in my relationship with this issue. I was aware, however, that telling at any point in my career could adversely affect my future career, and I did not want, early on to burn all the bridges to the EEOC.
>
> As I said, I may have used poor judgment. Perhaps I should have taken angry or even militant steps, both when I was in the agency or after I left it. But I must confess to the world that the course that I took seemed the better as well as the easier approach.
>
> I declined any comment to newspapers, but later, when Senate staff asked me about these matters, I felt I had a duty to report.
>
> I have no personal vendetta against Clarence Thomas. I seek only to provide the committee with information which it may regard as relevant.

It would have been more comfortable to remain silent. I took no initiative to inform anyone. But when I was asked by a representative of this committee to report my experience, I felt that I had to tell the truth. I could not keep silent.[23]

Judge Thomas denied Professor Hill's allegations. In his opening statement, Thomas describes his relationship with Hill as appropriately professional, apologizes to her for anything that may have been misconstrued by her as harassment, and refers to his career as one in which he had strongly condemned sexual harassment. He concludes the statement thus:

I have experienced the exhilaration of new heights from the moment I was called to Kennebunkport by the President to have lunch and he nominated me. That was the high point. At that time I was told, eye to eye, that, Clarence, you made it this far on merit; the rest is going to be politics. And it surely has been. . . .

Instead of understanding and appreciating the great honor bestowed upon me, I find myself here today defending my name, my integrity, because somehow select portions of confidential documents dealing with this matter were leaked to the public.

Mr. Chairman, I am a victim of this process. My name has been harmed. My integrity has been harmed. My character has been harmed. My family has been harmed. My friends have been harmed. There is nothing this committee,

THANK YOU FOR YOUR INTEREST IN BOOKS FROM THE PILGRIM PRESS.

Title of book purchased _____

What comments do you have? _____

Why did you purchase this book? (Check all that apply)

❑ Subject ❑ Recommendation of a friend ❑ Information on cover ❑ Gift
❑ Author ❑ Recommendation of reviewer ❑ Appearance of cover ❑ Other

If purchased: Bookseller _____ City _____ State _____

I am interested in the following subjects (check all that apply):

❑ African American Resources ❑ Evangelism and Church Growth ❑ Personal Growth/Spirituality
❑ Biblical Studies ❑ Lectionary and Worship ❑ Seasonal Resources
❑ Children's Sermons ❑ Meditation and Devotion ❑ United Church of Christ Identity
❑ Confirmation/Baptism ❑ Multicultural/Multiracial   and History
❑ Education: Christian, Theological ❑ Pastoral Resources ❑ CURRENT CATALOG

Name _____ Phone _____
Date _____ Fax _____
Address _____ City, State & Zip _____
_____ E-mail address _____

BOOKS AT THE NEXUS OF RELIGION AND CULTURE

THE PILGRIM PRESS

700 Prospect Avenue ■ Cleveland, Ohio 44115
Phone: 1-800-537-3394 ■ Fax: 1-216-736-2206
E-mail: pilgrim@ucc.org ■ Web sites: www.pilgrimpress.com

CALL OUR TOLL-FREE NUMBER, LOG ON TO OUR WEB SITE,
OR VISIT YOUR LOCAL BOOKSTORE.

this body, or this country can do to give me my good name back. Nothing.

I will not provide the rope for my own lynching, or for further humiliation. I am not going to engage in discussions, nor will I submit to roving questions, of what goes on in the most intimate parts of my private life, or the sanctity of my bedroom. These are the most intimate parts of my privacy, and they will remain just that: private.[24]

In Judge Thomas' second statement he adamantly denied the allegations again, and this time he drew explicit connections between his conservative politics and racism. He said: "And from my standpoint, as a black American, it is a high-tech lynching for uppity blacks who in any way deign to think for themselves, to do for themselves, to have different ideas, and it is a message that unless you kowtow to an old order, this is what will happen to you. You will be lynched, destroyed, caricatured by a committee of the U.S. Senate rather than hung from a tree."[25]

Many public conversations and published responses by African American jurists, public officials, scholars, and activists ensued. Prominent African Americans as individuals and members of organizations were already engaged—before Anita Hill's allegations—in either endorsing or opposing the appointment of Judge Thomas because of his conservative legal positions on issues such as affirmative action. This event is an example of a complex but discernable way in which African American sexual-gender relations can perpetuate ideas that sustain sexual-gender oppression in the African American community and consequently support the racist-patriarchal-capitalist oppression of African Americans in society.

Below I will offer a discussion of the Thomas-Hill event as an illustration of this. Two volumes, *Court of Appeal: The Black Community Speaks Out on the Racial and Sexual Politics of Thomas vs. Hill* (1992) and *Race-ing Justice, En-gendering Power: Essays on Anita Hill, Clarence Thomas, and the Construction of Social Reality* (1992), are the sources of diverse opinions that inform my discussion. Although there are many important issues deriving from this event (for example, political conservatism among African Americans, respect for diversity of intellectual and political positions among African Americans, the politics of the confirmation process itself, etc.) that are discussed in these volumes, my discussion below is narrowly focused on the issue of sexual-gender relations from the perspective of this chapter's analysis of the dynamics of such within the African American community.

How is the Hill-Thomas event illustrative of the dynamics of sexual-gender relations in the African American experience and its social reproduction of racist-patriarchal-capitalist oppression? The Hill-Thomas event reminds us that in spite of the reality of African American women's and men's shared history of being lynched in this country, that history has been largely interpreted as a history of the unjust killing of black men who were alleged to have committed sexual crimes against white women. Thus, when Thomas uses lynching as the metaphor for his experience of the

Senate Judiciary Committee's confirmation process as the allegations by Hill are allowed into the record, he seeks to put the matter back on racial rather than sexual terms. After all, everyone in the African American community (including or most especially women) should know that race trumps gender. Thus, when Hill makes her allegations public she can be branded a race traitor who is an ally of white racism.[26] Here was the crux of the matter for African Americans: A black woman betrayed the race by *publicly* accusing a black man of sexual impropriety. In a white racist society, even if Thomas had done what Hill said, Hill should not have spoken of it in mixed racial company. Perhaps, supportive of this last statement is the fact that in their position statement the Southern Christian Leadership Conference, the civil rights organization founded by Martin Luther King Jr. and other black ministers, supported the confirmation of Thomas without any mention of or attention to Hill's allegations.[27] Perhaps nothing should be inferred from the statement's silence regarding Hill, but it is clear from the content of the statement that race/racism is still the most critical barrier to black people's full participation in society.

From a social constructionist perspective, Hill and Thomas are actors in a sociohistorically derived racial sexual-gender drama that complicates the ability of either of these two persons to act as individuals as well as to be responded to as such. In the context of the confirmation hearing, Hill and Thomas stand before the Senate Committee as individuals but they are perceived (perhaps mostly unconsciously) as members of their racial sexual-gender social groups by the Committee and the African American community. As an individual, Hill seeks to regain some sense of self by manifesting belated courage by breaking her silence about the sexual harassment; as an individual, Thomas seeks to be heard as one who is entitled to be politically conservative amidst largely liberal African Americans and to be believed because of his professional history of support for women against sexual harassment. As members of their racial sexual-gender groups, the Committee perceives both Hill and Thomas through white racist objectification of their sexuality that West describes in the quote above; she is some strange combination of Jezebel and Aunt Jemima, and he is some equally weird mixture of Jack Johnson and Uncle Tom. To the African American community, Hill and Thomas represent the unresolved antagonism between black women and men that exists in the wake of the degeneration of the black civil rights agenda into the struggle for manhood that hooks describes in the previous quote. Toni Morrison sums up these matters eloquently:

> Anita Hill's description of Thomas's behavior toward her did not ignite a careful search for the truth; her testimony simply produced an exchange of racial tropes. Now it was he, the nominee, who was in danger of moving from "natural servant" to "savage demon," and the force of the balance of the confirmation process

was to reorder these signifying fictions. Is he lying or is she? Is he the benevolent one and she the insane one? Or is he the date raper, sexual assaulter, the illicit sexual signal, and she the docile, loyal servant? Those two major fictions, either/or, were blasted and tilted by a factual thing masquerading as a true thing: lynching. Being a fact of both white history and black life, lynching is also the metaphor of itself. While the mythologies about black personae debauched the confirmation process for all time, the history of black life was appropriated to elevate.[28]

What insights from Thomas vs. Hill thus inform this analysis of sexual-gender relations in the African American church? The Thomas vs. Hill event stands as a reminder that in order for African American sexual-gender relations not to do the shadow work that reproduces racist, patriarchal, capitalist objectification of black sexuality, there must be intracommunal accountability about those relations. The appropriation of black life in a manner that colludes with racist-patriarchal-capitalist oppression happens—whether or not African American women and men choose for such to happen. Consequently, the choices that African American women and men make about their sexual-gender relations impact both themselves individually and as members of their racial sexual-gender social groups. If there is some "agenda" for black liberation (and I hope there is a multifaceted and strategically pluralistic one), then surely it must be one that includes self-critical and con-structive dialogue about how not to be pawns of white racist sexual-gender objectification and how to act as subjects of sexual-gender self-actualization individually and sexual-gender justice communally. The African American church, as a social institution and human community that socializes women and men to partici-pate in both black life and society at large, is one place where such self-criticism and constructive dialogue must take place.

DIALOGUE ONE
A GROUP EXERCISE IN SOCIAL MYTH ANALYSIS

What is your first reaction to the following statements?

- Black women are confrontational.

- Black men are irresponsible.

- Black women are more bossy and domineering that other women.

- Black men are more physically aggressive than other men.

(A) When you read these statements, what sexual-gender social myths about African American women and men come to mind? Make a list of these myths. Compare and contrast the group's list with those presented in this chapter. What do you think of the nineteenth-century racial sexual-gender social mythology presented in this chapter? Do you see the myths that you have listed as deriving from that mythology? If so, in what ways? If not, why not?

(B) From whom and/or in what context did you learn sexual-gender myths? What do you think about the discussion of Wyatt's and Frank's descriptions of how African American women and men have adapted psychologically and internalized their sexual-gender myths in this chapter?

(C) Do you think that the African American church teaches and/or socializes (intentionally or unintentionally) women and men into sexual-gender myths that perpetuate sexual-gender oppression and subvert sexual-gender justice?

3

STANDING IN YET OUTSIDE THE GATES

The African American
Church as a Site of
Sexual-Gender Oppression
(A Womanist Assessment
of the Black Church
Since Frazier)

Within the church and without, African-American women and men are competing for life. This competition is a cruel wager on scarce resources in a hegemonic culture and social structure. Playing this wager means settling for an imposed hierarchy in which only one gender's concern is addressed at a time. The result is a praxeological disaster and an endangered community. A community affirms the worth of the people who are in it and invites others to join it because it offers life and health. To set up a hierarchy of needs based on femaleness and maleness is shortsighted and discriminatory. This lives out the model of the white power structure and the white version of Christianity that condones oppression.[1]

—Emilie M. Townes

It is important for black men to realize that women's liberation is a viable issue. We must recognize it and help others in the church to treat it seriously. It is not a joke. To get others to accept it as an issue that deserves serious consideration and discussion is the first step. As ministers in the church, how we treat the issue will affect the attitudes of others in our pastoral care. I realize that many women will give the appearance of accepting the place set aside for them by men as is true of many blacks in relation to whites. But just as whites were responsible for creating the societal structures that aided black self-hate, so black men are responsible for creating a similar situation among black women in the church. Saying that women like their place is no different from saying that blacks like theirs.[2]

—James H. Cone

It has not helped the cause of gender equity that the chief autonomous institution Black America has run throughout most of its history and which therefore may be the subconscious model for many Black institutions is the Black church. Most modern religion has an intimate relationship with patriarchy, and the Black church is no exception. The Black church simultaneously came to deliver the captives and was based on biblical teachings such as 'all wickedness is but little to the wickedness of a woman' (1 Corinthians 11:3) and that 'the head of every man is Christ, and the head of the woman is the man' (1 Peter 3:1). From the start, Black churches invariably were dominated by men who served as pastors, evangelists and deacons; and as visits to most Black churches reveal every Sunday, the Black church remains a female space dominated by men.[3]

— Linda Faye Williams

SCENARIO A

They don't think that I can do anything but cook. I have an MBA from Atlanta University, and what do I do at this church every weekend? Cook! We had our annual meeting last night; did any of them hear me? No! Those same self-righteous deacons (all men, of course) don't want to do anything that is different; therefore, anything that will serve women's needs was not even allowed on the floor for discussion. The only time that they think of us is when they want to raise some money by selling food. I keep telling myself that this is the last weekend that I will cook at this church, but then Sister Frances comes and asks me with that sad face of hers and here I am. I have some friends who are financial planners and investment counselors that I wanted to invite to the church to do some workshops with us to help us think of other ways to raise funds other than the sisters frying chicken every weekend, but no one wanted to hear my suggestions. Sister Frances may be right; the only way to get something done in this church is to put the idea into a man's mind and let him present it as if it were his idea.

SCENARIO B

They say there are five thousand people in this room—the largest ballroom of any hotel in Washington, D.C. Here we are pressed together, not even three inches between chairs. I wonder what happened to the air conditioning? Maybe there are too many people in this space to even feel a small breeze. What are they doing now? Another vote! It's 4:00 o'clock in the morning.

Forty years to get to this point. It's so hot I can't keep my mind on what they are saying or doing. The last vote did not elect a bishop. I want to keep my eyes open, but they're closing. Can't let them close. All I see when they are closed is a large crowd of people hugging me when I was first ordained. I must keep my mind on the present. "We will vote starting with the last Episcopal area." Now I have to wait through eleven Episcopal districts before I can vote.

I must keep smiling. People are looking at me. They don't understand! I've struggled, fought, bled, didn't die, forty years . . . Forty years for what? To be a bishop in a church that still does not respect women's leadership? Why do I even want to try. Oh, so hot! District four is voting. On the day of my ordination, someone said then that I could be the first woman bishop in the church. I didn't know if I would even get an appointment. When I did get an appointment, they gave me excuses year after year about my having to stay at the first little assignment. Everyone else (male) in my ordinand class was moved the second year, but there I sat. Someone told me it was a good appointment for a "woman." And if I really wanted to get moved, I needed to do something real special with the appointment I had. So I worked hard, tripled membership, increased the budget, married folk, buried folk, added a Christian education building, but still I sat. After fifteen years I finally figured out that no one cared whether I moved or not. They knew they were wrong leaving me there so long, that's why they eventually made me a presiding elder. Not a large district like the brothers in my class, but something I could "build" they said. So I built, increased the number of churches on the district, raised the budget, gave without question any amount the bishop asked for, but there I sat.

And now, here I am sitting again. Nothing really happening. Tally from the last vote is being read, I hear my name, 175 votes. Only 175 people here think I should be elected a bishop. There are over 700 delegates; only 175 people think that I have given, served, worked well with and for the church? How can that be? I have participated in everything and kept my head above all the scandal. I gave of my life unselfishly, even sacrificially, to the church for the past forty years. I have prepared myself for this moment, spiritually, and as a student and a strong advocate for church programs. What do they want? I've been careful about my personal appearance, just like the older elders told me. I married, had children, acted in the ways "becoming a woman of God"; what more? District two is voting. I must get myself together; they must not think that I'm upset by the small number of votes I've received thus far. The preacher on my left is trying to say something to me. I can't seem to focus. I know he's patting my leg and saying something about "chin up." Someone behind me is saying we need to finish this voting so we can all go to bed, and why don't they stop voting for that woman, "they know she isn't going to win, and we could all get some sleep." "District one, stand!" We're going to the voting booths. My legs don't want to move; I stand with only sheer will holding my legs up. We vote. We cram ourselves back into those small chairs. The tally is ready quickly. The tally is read. What happened to my name? I don't hear it. Shouts begin to ring out, we've elected a bishop; his name is . . .

SCENARIO C

Girl, I'm so lucky. My pastor is not one of those "can't stand women ministers" people. Just last Sunday he announced that Jackie and I will be ordained this year after a special class with him this summer. So many women can't even speak from the pulpits of their churches.

From the very first moment that I told him that I believed the Lord was calling me to preach, he's been right in my corner. He immediately allowed me to lead worship and teach Sunday School. I feel so badly about my sisters who have leaders that won't let them participate at all. My pastor supports me all along the way. He even found $300 for books when I enrolled in seminary.

My pastor just wants me to be the best that I can be —that's why he didn't recommend me for ordination immediately after completing my M.Div. degree. Instead, for the past four years, he's involved me in all phases of the work of the church; I've taught Sunday school, led Bible study, instructed the new members, and directed the children's choir. It's been a long time coming, ten years actually, but this year my pastor is going to let it be known that I'm ready to be an associate pastor or the pastor of a small church.

SCENARIO D

The visiting preacher, a brawny brown man with smooth skin and teeth made of pearl, was coming to the close of his sermon, a ritual moment of climax in the black church. It is the inevitable point to which the entire service builds. Its existence is the only justification for the less dramatic rites of community—greeting visitors, collecting tithes, praying for the sick, reading scripture, and atoning for sins. These rites are a hallway to the sanctuary of zeal and vision formed by the black sermon. . . .

"We've got to keep o-o-o-o-on," he tunefully admonished. The preceding wisdom of his oration on Christian sexuality, arguing the link between passion and morality, turned this cliche into sermonic clincher.

"We can't give up," he continued. "Because we've got God, oh yes, we've got Go-o-o-o-od, un-humh, on our side."

"Yes," members of the congregation shouted. The call and response between the pulpit and the pew escalated as each spurred the other on in ever changing rounds of emotion.

"We've got a friend who will never forsake us."

"Yes sir, Reverend."

"We've got a God who can make a way outta no way."

"Yes we do."

"He's a heart fixer, and a mind regulator."

"Oh, yes he is."

"I'm here tonight to tell you whatever moral crisis you're facin,' God can fix it for you."

"Thank you, Jesus."

"If you're facin' trouble on the job, God can make your boss act better."

"Tell the truth, Reverend."

"If your kids won't act right, God can turn them around."

"Hallelujah!"

"If you're fornicating, and I know some of y'all been fornicatin,' God can turn lust to love and give you a healthier relationship with Him."

"Hold your hope! Hold your hope!"

"If you're committin' adultery, and I know some of y'all are doing that, too, God can stop your rovin' eyes and keep you from messin' up. Won't he do it, church?"

"Yes! Yes he will!"

"If your marriage is fallin' apart, and there's no joy—I said there's no jo-oy-oy at your address, God can do for you what he did for David. David asked God: 'Restore unto me the joy of thy Salvation.' I am a witness tonight, children. God can do that, church. God can restore your joy. Won't he do it, children?!

"Yes he will! Thank you, Jesus! Thank you, Jesus!"

"I'm closing now, but before I go, I just stopped by to let you know that you can't find salvation in things. You can't find salvation in your wife or husband. And you certainly can't find salvation in sex. Did y'all hear me? You can't find salvation in sex. You can't find it in sleepin' around, tryin' to fill the empty places of your life with pleasure and loose livin.'"

"Thank you, Jesus!"

"You can only find salvation in our Lord and Savior, Jesus Christ! Do y'all hear me? Jesus, that's who you need! Jesus, that's who can save you. Jesus, the author and finisher of our faith. Jesus! Jesus! Jesus!

"Thank ya! Oh, Hallelujah."

After the service was over, after the worshipers had time to greet and thank the preacher, we ministers, five in all, retired to the pastor's study.

As a young minister in my early twenties, I was just glad to be in their number, bonding with ministerial mentors, men standing on the front line of spiritual warfare, or as the black church memorably refers to it, "standing in the gap": carrying and crying the judgment of the Almighty, opening opportunity for salvation, proclaiming the soul's rescue and the requirements of redemption, and edifying believers with the inscrutable, wholly uncompromising, tell-it-like-it-is, to-be-preached-in-season-and-out-of-season gospel of the living God. I was simply enjoying this magical moment of fraternal friendliness. And it was just that. No women were there. No one thought it odd that they weren't. We never remarked once on their absence, and indeed, we counted on their absence to say things, manly things, that we couldn't, didn't dare say in mixed company. Still, I wasn't prepared for what followed.

"Revrun, I need to ask you something," the visiting preacher begged the pastor. His eyebrows were raised, a knowing look was on his face, and his voice affected, if not quite a mock seriousness, then a naughty whisper that clued us that his curiosity was more carnal than cerebral.

"Who is that woman with those big breasts who was sitting on the third aisle to my left?" he eagerly inquired. "Damn, she kept shouting and jiggling so much I almost lost my concentration."

"She is a fine woman, now," the pastor let on.

"Well, doc, do you think you could fix me up with her?" The visiting preacher asked with shameless lust.

"I'll see what I can do, Revrun," the pastor promised.[4]

SCENARIO E

I wasn't trying to hide who I am. At least I don't think I was. I've been a part of this denomination all of my life. I grew up in this area. My pastor wrote my recommendations for seminary. I served on many committees and boards at different levels of the church. Now my presiding elder wants to act as if he really wasn't sure of my sexual identity until I did the union service for two lesbian women in the church. It's funny—I didn't do the service because I am lesbian, I did that service because I believe that homosexual persons should have the opportunity to make that kind of commitment. My presiding elder says that my action was an act of blasphemy against the church and that it finally gave me away, allowing him to be sure of my identity. And now that he is sure of my identity, he must report me to the bishop and let him know that I am in violation of church law. It appears that if I had never done the service or acted in any way different than anyone else, I would have been allowed to continue to pastor. What does that mean? Is there really a law? I remember the bishops in one of their letters to the church affirming what they call the biblical view of homosexuality as a sin against God. There really isn't a law in the *Book of Discipline*. The *Discipline* talks about behavior befitting a pastor. I think that my behavior is that of a pastor. My sexual identity does not impair my ability to pastor.

Questions for reflection:

> What happens when the dynamics of sexual-gender relations described in chapter two are practiced in the church?

> In what ways are the structures of relationships between men and women (structures of labor, power, and desire) outlined in chapter one operative when the church is a site of sexual-gender oppression?

> How can women and men in the church become accountable for dismantling sexual-gender oppression rather than acting in complicity with such?

In this chapter I turn to the ways in which the church is a site of sexual-gender oppression. I use the term "site" to signify that the African American church is being examined as "a particular context that shapes the encounters" between African American men and women into practices that promote the subordination of women by men. In other words, it is the particularity of the context, particular sociohistorical and sociopsychological experiences (as described in chapter 2), that foments present sexual-gender oppression in the African American church. Also, by focusing on the site of oppression in terms of encounters, this analysis presupposes that these encounters can be renegotiated so as to restructure the relations of oppression into liberating ones for each of the parties to the encounter. Finally, the aim of this chapter is to disclose the socioethical dilemma at the heart of this oppression and how it impacts the character and agency of the church and its members.

In 1964 a book by African American sociologist E. Franklin Frazier entitled *The Negro Church in America* was published. In that book, Frazier described the Negro church as "a nation within a nation." The "nation within a nation" metaphor signified the way that the church functioned for Negroes. The church was the means for stabilizing moral and family life; it was the place for establishing an institutional economic base, nurturing educational achievement, and fulfilling political aspirations in a society that denied Negroes full participation in its social, economic, educational, and political life. Indeed, according to Frazier, the Negro church, an agency of social control and assimilation, was a "refuge in a hostile white world."[5]

Ten years later, another African American sociologist of religion and social ethicist, C. Eric Lincoln, was commissioned to write an appraisal of Franklin's work in light of the significant changes in African American life in the wake of the civil rights movement of the sixties. In the introduction to his book, *The Black Church Since Frazier*, Lincoln writes:

> The Negro Church is dead because the norms and the presuppositions which structured and conditioned it are not the relevant norms and presuppositions to which contemporary Blacks who represent the future of religion in the Black community can give their asseveration and support. The Black Church is or must become the characteristic expression of institutionalized religion for contemporary Black Americans because it is the perfect counterpart

of the Black man's present self-perception and the way he sees God and man, particularly the white man, in a new structuring of relationships from which he emerges freed of the traditional proscriptions that compromised his humanity and limited his hope.[6]

From Lincoln's perspective, the black church that emerged from the significant moral, political, and economic efforts for racial justice during the sixties had a distinctive edge from its predecessor, the "Negro church." The black church was now being led by *men* who were no longer taking their cues from the white man ("freed of the traditional proscriptions that compromised his humanity and limited his hope"). After all, the civil rights efforts of the sixties had a double-edged quality. There were efforts based in moral suasion and economic reform under leaders such as the Reverend Drs. Martin Luther King Jr. (the Montgomery Bus Boycott and founding of the Southern Christian Leadership Conference) and Leon Sullivan (the "selective patronage" campaign in Philadelphia and founding of Opportunities for Industrialization Centers)—efforts aimed at full integration in U.S. society. There was also the cry for "Black Power" by young militants of the Student Nonviolent Coordinating Committee along with the articulation of a black theology of liberation, self-definition and self-determination "by any means necessary"—efforts aimed at radically disrupting the social, political, and economic structures of U.S. society. According to Lincoln, the black church was born thus:

Amid the crunching of night sticks, the snarling of dogs, the screaming of epithets, the barring of Black Christians from white churches, and the escalating murder of Blacks who protested it all, the white Church as a point of spiritual reference lost its luster, and the Negro Church, which had accommodated itself to the notion of a superior morality (however obscure) in the white man's expression of their common faith, now thoroughly disillusioned, consigned itself to its own history. The Black Church as a self-conscious, self-assertive, inner-directed institution was born, but as the Black Church is not the Negro Church reborn, neither is it the white Church replicated. And yet in some sense it is both of these. Ironically, the white Church in America is the principal *raison d'etre* for the Black Church, for just as the white Church permitted and tolerated the Negro Church, it made the Black Church necessary for a new generation of Black people who refuse to be "Negroes" and who are not impressed by whatever it means to be white. [7]

This description of the black church is compelling and valid to a point. However, as I discussed in chapter 2, the shift into a more militant black consciousness during the latter years of the civil rights movement was accompanied by a shift into a militant patriarchal consciousness. The black church was not immune from this shift. Indeed, the point of departure for my womanist assessment in this chapter is this:

The Black church since Frazier has functioned as a "surrogate world"[8] wherein African American men as clergy have perceived themselves as securing the rights of patriarchal privilege denied them elsewhere. At last, as the "father" of the household of God,[9] African American men are able to garner the respect of and dominance over women that some maintain that they have not been granted in the larger society, and consequently cannot achieve even in their own homes.

This is a harsh point of departure. However, I do think that numbers of African American women and men would bear witness to its validity if they could be honest with themselves about sexual-gender relations within the African American church. In the surrogate world of the church, African Americans have maintained a place of refuge and development for oppressed black people in a white racist, capitalist world —not a refuge from a hostile white racist, patriarchal, capitalist world. But why is this the case? Why is it that a church that has been a leader in the quest for racial and economic justice has been far less able (willing?) to maintain sexual-gender justice within its own walls as well as to connect the dots between the quest for racial and economic justice with sexual-gender justice in society?

Sociologist and womanist Cheryl Townsend Gilkes offers some of the most provocative analyses of the complexity and duplicity of the black church with respect to matters of gender. Insights from her analysis in the essay, "The Roles of Church and Community Mothers: Ambivalent American Sexism or Fragmented African Familyhood?"[10] and "The Politics of 'Silence':

Dual-Sex Political Systems and Women's Traditions of Conflict"[11] are especially helpful. Gilkes's query as to whether the sexual-gender relations in the church attest to an "ambivalent American sexism or fragmented African familyhood?" stems from an explication of the "great prestige" and "real authority" of church and community "mothers." These mothers are role models, respected elders, and/or power brokers through the relatively autonomous women's organizations within the church. According to Gilkes, herein lies the fragmented African familyhood: the role and functions of church mothers seem derivative of a West African legacy of independent womanhood (for example, women who controlled the market places and provided leadership in religious groups) that is reminiscent of West African familial organization and the dual-sex politics of such (for example, women's political organizations of wives of a lineage). Also, consistent with this legacy of independent African womanhood, Gilkes asserts that black women have maintained "traditions of conflict" and "organized resistance to patriarchy within the black religious experience." Two examples of this are "a tradition of biblical feminism"[12] and the establishment of Women's Day.[13]

Ambivalent American sexism is evident when men invoke "sexist ideology stemming from white patriarchal historical traditions." Gilkes describes what happens in two particular denominational contexts when men invoke this sexist ideology in the church:

> In the sacred world of the black Baptist and Methodist denominations, women are con-

fronted with the ideology of the Pauline epistles, women's physical inability to preach in a
dramatic, energetic, and celebrative style, or
the problems posed by pregnancy. In a world
where "the call" is seen as something reserved
strictly for men, black women preachers are
sharply and persistently questioned. Sometimes
it is implied that a sincere "call" has, by definition, a detrimental effect on the black woman
preacher's sexuality. It is in such settings that
black women, particularly those called to ministry, confront a complex of attitudes and ide-
ologies through which black men define their
prerogatives . . . [14]

The impact of this ambivalent American sexism is
not only the exclusion of women from ordained ministry; its assault upon women's personhood and her authentic status as a minister is forcefully illustrated by the
following remarks of an established African American
clergywoman:

Then, the revivalist came out and thanked God
for . . . the presence of all the brother preachers; and, then invited all the brother preachers
to stand. Sitting in the pew, I was immediately
confronted with a crisis of identity. Which do I
own, my call or my gender? Do I sit and deny
this call, this claim of God on my life decreed by
God before I was formed in the womb? Do I sit
and now again, another time add to my own
history of shame, for the years I tried to do

everything else but answer this call? Or do I stand and deny my gender? A preacher I am, a brother I am not. I finally resolved the violent conflict by standing. Because, when I stood I stood as I am. I stood in the total authenticity of my being—black preacher, Baptist, woman. For the same God who made me a preacher is the same God who made me a woman. And, I am convinced that God was not confused on either count.[15]

Thus, in my words, women stand in, yet outside, the gates of the black church; they control relatively autonomous women's departments of the church but their authority in other spheres of the church's life and acceptance in leadership roles must be negotiated and approved by male gatekeepers. Consequently, the paradoxical coexistence of a women's tradition of resistance and male gatekeepers stands at the heart of the complexity and duplicity of sexual-gender relations in the African American church and tends to lead the leadership and the membership to dismiss or excuse the ways that sexual-gender oppression occurs in the church. A look at the scenarios opening this chapter can make this point more clear.

ANALYSIS OF SCENARIOS

The scenarios at the beginning of this chapter point to how the structures of labor, power, and desire that secure male domination play out in the church. Recall scenario A. Women are responsible for raising money by executing a task that is traditionally considered women's work, cooking. When one woman speaks up at an annual church meeting with alternative suggestions for fund raising, she is apparently not heard. Sister Frances then reminds the frustrated woman that she must put her idea into a man's mind and let him present it. When women are relegated to tasks that are associated with traditional notions of women's work and their ideas are disallowed because they are uttered by women, sexual-gender oppression is occurring.

Likewise, when the formal process for being appointed or called to a pastorate, or the formal process for ordination or election to a governing board of the church (such as the episcopacy) become circuitous and convoluted for women but men are treated fairly, given an advantage by being promoted sooner, or may even bypass the formal process as is the case in scenarios B and C, sexual-gender oppression is occurring.

The structure of desire is most evident in scenarios D and E, although it is present in the other scenarios as a latent source of the antagonism toward the men or submissive compliance with any and all expectations that derive from the women's experiences of being unheard in scenario A and disadvantaged through derisive application of requirements in scenarios B and C. In scenario D the revival preacher enlists the help of another male preacher to secure a liaison with a woman in the congregation, someone he does not know but toward whom he feels sexually attracted. Although the young preacher present is surprised by this request, the other more senior ministers are not. This suggests that the revival preacher's request is seen as permissible (if not normative) to this male clergy peer group. Sexual-gender oppression is occurring in this instance because there is a pattern of behavior (tacitly if not explicitly) condoning the sexual use of women by a group of men who are abusing the power afforded them by their pastoral office.

In scenario E the structure of desire is operative on personal and institutional levels. Apparently, the female pastor in this scenario has met the official requirements for ordination and has been judged qualified to pastor a congregation. She has been an active and seemingly respected member of her denomination. Out of her convictions (which derive in part from who she is as well as how she understands her call to ministry), she performs a pastoral duty, a union service (a marriage) for a lesbian couple. The presiding elder, as the representative for institutional interests, concludes that the pastor's performance of the service amounts to confession of her homosexual identity and violation of the church's law. When there is a disjunction between personal values and the sexual identity of the pastor and institutional standards with respect to those values and identity, yet this disjunction is accommodated as long as silence is kept, sexual-gender oppression is occurring as standards that claim to regulate the ministerial office are applied to the personhood of an individual whose action has not fundamentally violated the standards of that office. Thus, it is the sexual identity of the pastor, not sexual misconduct or the breaking of church law, that is actually the offense.

With these scenarios as just explicated in mind, the answer to the question about why the black church since Frazier has not been a refuge from a hostile white racist, patriarchal, capitalist world is the values inconsistency at the center of its institutional ethos. While justice is a core value of the black church with respect to racist, capitalist oppression, that core value is subverted when men assert patriarchal privilege. Patriarchal privilege has "control of women" as its core value, and this value cannot exist in the same context in which justice is a core value without creating a context that breeds moral corruption.[16] Moral corruption here refers to the inconsistency between the black church's steadfast pursuit of justice with respect to racial and economic oppression while not pursuing sexual-gender justice, and consequently becoming a site of sexual-gender oppression. In the church as the site of sexual-gender oppression, moral corruption is also manifest in the behavior of its members in that they lack integrity (a point that I will explicate more in the next chapter).

In fact, the African American church has developed a normative patriarchal institutional ethos that has transmuted the black church, a surrogate world for racially oppressed black people, into the African American church, a "protected space" for sexual-gender transgressions, a place where silence is kept about unethical—inappropriate and/or abusive—sexual contact or "sexualized behavior."[17] Sexual contact or sexualized behavior is unethical (inappropriate and/or abusive) when the relationship between those involved is one in which an imbalance of power exists. In other words, the relationship between a pastor and a layperson is an intrinsic relationship of asymmetrical power. When the pastor in scenario A in chapter 2 initiates a sexual relationship with the laywoman, unethical sexual contact occurs because the clergyman has power by virtue of his role as pastor that overwhelms the power of the laywoman by virtue of her status in relationship to his role and authority.

Moreover, in the context of the church as a site of sexual-gender oppression, women are not men's equals or even complements but are regarded and (mis)treated as men's subordinates, euphemistically referred to as supporters or the "backbone of the church." The male clergy person in scenario A assumes that it is his "right" as an ordained minister to seek the assistance of the female layperson in terms of both his professional tasks and personal nonsexual as well as sexual needs. The female layperson is perceived as (and she may even believe) fulfilling her "natural" role as she gives of her time and talent as well as her physical and emotional self to aid this male in his role as minister while also fulfilling his needs as a man. In the African American church as a site of sexual-gender oppression, this man and this woman enact prescribed roles for being male and female—sexual-gender scripts—into which they have been socialized according to the values operative in this context.

In the sexual-gender oppressive African American church, the values inconsistency—justice versus "control of women"—that stands at the heart of the church's moral life becomes the driving force behind why male clergy and laywomen have relationships that deny their own self-actualization (see opening quotes). This explains why the minister may preach about salvation and sexual impropriety and yet engage in relationships of sexual misconduct (Scenario D). It explains why church membership may perpetuate gender injustice by either denying women full participation in the governing authority of the church (Scenarios A and B) or church leadership imposing constraints that hinder access to ordination (Scenario C). It is why the sexual identity of the homosexual pastor is grounds to dismiss a pastor whose ministerial conduct is otherwise commendable or to rewrite church law in order to punish rather than maintain order, thus usurping pastoral authority that should be established both through the polity of the church and through the dictates of vocational conscience deriving from being called by God (Scenario E).

In this chapter, by referring to the African American church as a site of sexual-gender oppression, I have focused on the church as a social institution and human community. This focus has rendered an explication of the dynamics of sexual-gender relations in terms of the institutional practices and values that ground the church's sexual-gender oppression. Such sexual-gender oppressive practices (as shown in the scenarios) are lived out as encounters between women and men that manifest denial of self-actualization, exclusion from full participation in church governance or ordination, and punitive scrutiny of the homosexual pastor because of her/his sexual identity. These practices thus mark the church as a place of moral corruption wherein there is inconsistency between justice and "control of women" as a core value by which the church orders its life. The encounters between women and men in the church are then the result of socialization into sexual-gender scripts based in this values inconsistency and reinforce the context as one of moral corruption. In the final chapter, I will turn to the task of how the church might transform its moral life from one based in the moral corruption of sexual-gender oppression.

DIALOGUE TWO
AN EXERCISE IN CULTURAL AND RELIGIOUS CRITICISM[18]

Select a popular video that portrays relationships between black women and men (for example, *Waiting to Exhale* or *The Brothers*).

Before viewing the video, establish some ground rules, a covenant, for the dialogue, such as the following:

We agree to engage in this dialogue with

- CORDIALITY

- SENSITIVITY

- TOLERANCE

- RESPECT

    for the persons involved.

I understand that anything shared

- CONFIDENTIALLY WILL STAY IN THIS ROOM.

I desire to

- LEARN SOMETHING ABOUT MYSELF AND IMPROVE MY RELATIONSHIPS WITH OTHER WOMEN AND MEN.

After viewing the video together, begin your cultural and religious criticism by asking questions such as these:

- To what extent are the characters portrayed in the video stereotypical representations of African American women and men?

- To what extent are the behaviors presented in the video stereotypical?

- Is there any "truth" to the portrayal of characters and behaviors when they are analyzed as reflective of sexual-gender oppression as practiced through the encounters between African American women and men per the description of such in this chapter? Are there groups of women and men who are invisible to this portrayal of sexual-gender relations?

- How might women and men in the African American church who desire to promote accountability with regard to sexual-gender oppression respond to videos such as this one? (Answers might include: "It's just entertainment;" "We can learn something about ourselves and how the larger society continues to perceive us;" "So what?")

OUR HOPE IS BUILT ON . . .

Rudiments for Transforming
the Moral Life of the
African American Church

Now the whole group of those who believed were of one heart and soul, and no one claimed private ownership of any possessions, but everything they owned was held in common. With great power the apostles gave their testimony to the resurrection of the Lord Jesus, and great grace was upon them all. There was not a needy person among them, for as many as owned lands or houses sold them and brought the proceeds of what was sold. They laid it at the apostles' feet, and it was distributed to each as any had need. There was a Levite, a native of Cyprus, Joseph, to whom the apostles gave the name Barnabas (which means 'son of encouragement'). He sold a field that belonged to him, then brought the money, and laid it at the apostles' feet.

But a man named Ananias, with the consent of his wife Sapphira, sold a piece of property. With his wife's knowledge, he kept back some of the proceeds, and brought only a part and laid it at the apostles' feet. "Ananias," Peter asked, "why has Satan filled your heart to lie to the Holy Spirit and to keep back part of the proceeds of the land? While it remained unsold, did it not remain your own? And after it was sold, were not the proceeds at your disposal? How is it that you have contrived this deed in your heart? You did not lie to us but to God!" Now when Ananias heard these words, he fell down and died. And great fear seized all who heard of it. The young men came and wrapped up his body, then carried him out and buried him.

After an interval of about three hours his wife came in, not knowing what had happened. Peter said to her, "Tell me whether you and your husband sold the land for such and such a price." And she said, "Yes, that was the price." Then Peter said to her, "How is it that you have agreed together to put the Spirit of the Lord to the test? Look, the feet of those who have buried your husband are at the door, and they will carry you out." Immediately she fell down at his feet and died. When the young men came in they found her dead, so they carried her out and buried her beside her husband. And great fear seized the whole church and all who heard of these things.

—Acts 4:32–5:11 NRSV

Questions for reflection:

A moral vision is an overarching ethical frame of reference that indicates what is good and evil, acceptable and unacceptable, responsible and irresponsible with respect to character and agency.

> What are some features of a moral vision for the church suggested by this passage of scripture? What happens to undermine the moral vision?

> Using your moral imagination (the capacity of heart of mind in dialogue to perceive images of moral life), make a list of images for the church's moral life that this passage evokes for you.

> What images ground a liberated relationship between women and men?

> The role morality of clergy (the values and norms practiced by men or women in their role as ordained ministers)?

> The relationship between clergy and laity?

"Are all the ministers and preachers blameless in life and character?" Near the conclusion of each Annual Conference of the African Methodist Episcopal Zion (AMEZ) Church that question from the Discipline is asked; it marks that point in the conference referred to as "the passing of character." In the annual conferences of which I was a member, this question was the signal for all ordained persons to assemble at the altar before the bishop and the body of elected delegates. The

bishop then asks if anyone has a charge against the character of any of the clergy at the altar. Hearing no
charges, the bishop offers words of encouragement,
shakes each minister's hand, and dismisses us with "our
characters passed" for another year.

In the thirteen years that I was an AMEZ clergy
person and a participant in annual conferences in more
than one part of the country, I never heard a charge
brought before the conference during this time of in-
quiry as to whether or not our characters should be
passed. Even when there were allegations of clergy sexual or fiscal misconduct of which everyone was aware,
there was an inability to face forthrightly (individually
or communally) this misconduct. I think that this inability to face forthrightly such conduct is a problem in
most denominations, and so I have not singled out the
AMEZ denomination for some special criticism. However, this inability, a failure of moral courage, is particularly disturbing in light of the African American
church's public witness with respect to racial and economic social justice struggles. That public witness is
morally corrupted when the moral life of the church—
its sexual-gender, clergy, and ministerial ethics—is not
equally characterized by justice.

In this chapter I turn to the task of integrating the
analyses of the previous chapters through a constructive
proposal for transforming the moral life of the church.
I have opened this chapter with a text from the book of
Acts as the point of departure for this constructive proposal because it suggests a moral vision for the transformed church. Although biblical scholars mostly point
to the Acts text to describe the church's early life, as

one concerned with the sharing of economic resources as a critical feature of its common life, I am proposing that this text also speaks to the African American church today about a relationship between a vital communal economy, partnership between men and women, and the power of the Holy Spirit in the church and for the church's witness in society.

The moral vision contained within this passage of scripture is one that earmarks the economy of the church household as intrinsically related to the integrity of the church's members and the church's faithfulness to what the Spirit requires. When men and women in the church collude to lie about and withhold their full contribution to the church's economy, it is an act of spiritual transgression that threatens the lives of the individuals, the community, and, consequently, the ministry of the church to others outside its walls.

This text thus speaks to the African American church in a forceful way because this church has had and continues to have the quest for racial harmony and economic justice at the center of its moral vision, and both women and men are expected to live faithfully toward the fulfillment of the vision.

It is my contention, however, that when African American women and men act in complicity with sexual-gender injustice in the church, the church betrays its moral vision and corrupts both its internal moral life and its witness in the larger society. Such complicity between men (like Ananias) and women (like Sapphira) is willful hypocrisy against the Holy Spirit that is the power of the church. Breaking complicity with the moral corruption of sexual-gender injustice requires accountability on the part of clergy (like Peter) and laity (like those who remove the dead Ananias and Sapphira) who are willing to name the misconduct publicly so as to create a communal ethos of responsibility within the church that grounds its life and witness to others ("And great fear seized the whole church and all who heard of these things."). Having now presented the dynamics of African American sexual-gender relations (chapter 1) and exposed the ways in the African American church is a site of sexual-gender oppression (chapter 2), I turn in this final chapter to how women and men in the church are to be moral agents who move along the moral agency axis from complicity with sexual-gender injustice to accountability in naming such injustice to responsibility for creating sexual-gender justice in the church. The remainder of this chapter is a proposal for moving the African American church along the moral agency axis into responsibility for sexual-gender justice, thus transforming the moral life of the church.

SEXUAL-GENDER ETHICS

In chapter 1, I defined sexual-gender ethics as the morality (virtues, values, ideals, and norms) governing the relations between women and men who are biologically different beings (sexual) with socially constructed meanings of being female and male (gender) that they bring to both their private and public interactions. I use the hyphenated term sexual-gender to remind us of the need to be ever mindful of the interrelationship between biological difference and socially constructed meaning that is the crux of our being and doing as women and men. Thus far I have exposed the morality governing oppressive relations between African American women and men. This morality is earmarked by:

(1) blaming and counterblaming on the part of women and men for the ways that each fails to fulfill gender role expectations—such as women displaying femininity and unconditional support and men being providers and protectors;

(2) denial of self-actualization through psychological adaptation and behavior that is gullible and irresponsible on the part of women and exploitative and dismissive on the part of men; and

(3) abuse of clerical power by men and internalization of racist-patriarchal-capitalist objectification of black sexuality by women and men. African American women and men acting out of this morality within the black church are moral actors in a church that is a site of sexual-gender oppression and a supportive social institution of racist-patriarchal-capitalist oppression.

In order to transform the sexual-gender morality of African American women and men into one governing liberated relations, there must be counter-socialization of African American women and men with respect to sexual-gender social mythology and roles. What is socialization, and what will counter-socialization entail?

Sexual-gender socialization refers to the processes by which we acquire our sexual-gender myths and role expectations through those persons (such as parents and teachers) and institutions (such as schools, churches, and media) that are socializing agents. These processes are cognitive and behavioral; in other words, socialization refers to the ways that we learn to perceive and interpret expectations as well as to act with respect to gender. We may be socialized by being taught certain beliefs or through the role models for being women and men that are available for us to imitate. Importantly, through socialization we are given sexual-gender scripts.

In this discussion, I consider socialization a form of moral education whereby women and men acquire virtues and values associated with a sexual-gender morality. Although there are traditional or status-quo sexual-gender roles deriving from the sexual-gender morality, these roles can be changed because (1) the roles are learned—historically specific and relative, and (2) persons are moral beings (have the capacity to be intentional) who can challenge and resist traditional roles and expectations. Transforming the sexual-gender relations of African American women and men in the church will thus be accomplished through moral education that affects countersocialization.

This countersocialization may be understood as one way of practicing the ongoing process of resocialization that is at the heart of the Pauline project of communal ethics. Paul's communal ethics was based in "the power of the cross," the power of God, the power of life. Importantly, the power of the cross is the power of love, and a community formed by the power of the cross has two critical pillars: (1) unity and (2) mutual service.[1] Moreover, Paul understood that a community shaped by the power of the cross is one wherein its members acquire a new symbol system and meaning structure. The community's members acquire the new meaning structure by means of resocialization into a specifically Christian ethos; the resocialization is an ongoing process wherein "there will always be overlap between the old symbol system and the new, between old and new ways of perceiving and behaving."[2]

Moral education as sexual-gender countersocialization in the African American church must be such a process of resocialization. This moral education will entail nurturing moral postures among women and men that enable them to question what is normative when behavior is oppressive and to call for public accountability when sexual-gender oppression is exposed. The needful moral postures will be distinctive but complementary for the two sexual-gender groups. The moral posture for women will be oppositional but not antagonistic; for men, it will be self-critical but not self-denigrating. African American women operating from an oppositional but not antagonistic moral posture recognize that the expectations and behavior of African American men can perpetuate sexual-gender oppression. These women's moral agency will be oppositional because these women will not deny the sexual-gender injustice of the church and because they will exercise challenges to that injustice that are constructive rather then merely deconstructive. African American men have a self-critical but not self-denigrating moral posture when they acknowledge their assertion of patriarchal privilege over African American women in the context of the African American church. These men's moral agency will be self-critical but not self-denigrating when they recognize their gender-based power and seek to use that power for the creation of liberated sexual-gender relations, knowing that their personal power and manhood is not diminished by such action.

Nurturing these moral postures requires inculcating integrity in these women and men who are seeking finally to transform the moral corruption (the values inconsistency between justice and control of women based in patriarchal privilege) of the church as a site of sexual-gender oppression. According to Stephen Carter, integrity "demands a difficult process of discerning one's deepest understanding of right and wrong, and then further requires action consistent with what one has learned."[3] Integrity thus involves three steps. First, a person takes the time to discern right from wrong, acknowledging such even over and against what one believes. Second, the person resolves "to fight openly for what one believes to be true and right and good, even when there is risk to oneself." Third, the person is "willing to say that he or she is acting consistently with what he or she has decided as right." Also, integrity may consist in breaking the rules or reaching moral conclusions that differ from those of the majority, and it requires being open and public about the reasons for one's dissent and conclusions.[4] The importance of Carter's explication of integrity to this discussion is his emphasis on discernment as the beginning of integrity. The process of discerning right and wrong aligns with a notion of the social construction of sexual-gender morality. In other words, the task of moral education as counter-socialization is to foster a willingness to discern the rightness and wrongness of normative sexual-gender ethics even in the context of the church. For, "if we refuse to take the time for discernment, a discernment that might challenge cherished beliefs, then it is hard to see how we can ever construct a [sexual-gender ethics] of integrity."[5]

In order for moral education as sexual-gender countersocialization to be part of how the church fulfills it function as a social institution and human community that fosters sexual-gender justice, power imbalances in the church as a site of sexual-gender oppression must be addressed. The power imbalance between clergy and laity is at the center of such imbalances. Thus, the discussion now turns to clergy ethics.

CLERGY ETHICS

Clergy ethics refers to any formal (usually written) code of conduct prescribed for clergy or others acting in a ministerial role by a denomination and/or the role morality practiced by persons who are ordained to fulfill the role of clergy in the church. In this discussion, the emphasis has been on role morality rather than formal codes of conduct. The reason for this emphasis is the assumption that while the formulation of codes of conduct has been and is a significant way for the church to regulate sexual-gender morality in the church, such codes are actually limited in that they only control behavior.[6] The limited function of codes makes them ineffective in transforming the moral life of the church, the more needed, comprehensive aim of the church that seeks to be a site of sexual-gender justice. The discussion of clergy ethics is here therefore concerned with the role morality of clergy that is based upon how power is interpreted and enacted by clergy.

The practice(s) of power that drives sexual-gender in-justice is one wherein power is interpreted as a commodity that is possessed. When male clergy in the context of the church seek to possess the power of clerical status, they do so in one way by asserting heterosexual patriarchal privilege. The assertion of heterosexual patriarchal privilege is enacted by using lay women to fulfill personal and professional needs, dismissing or silencing the voices of women (lay and ordained) in the governing of the church, restricting or eliminating the full participation of women as leaders at various levels of the church's ministry, and denying the presence and legitimacy of homosexual persons as leaders and members. The practice(s) of power is dominating and controlling as it establishes and maintains a hierarchy of relations between sexual-gender groups, with heterosexual men at the top of the hierarchy. Groups of persons and practices are "normal," "legitimate," "acceptable," "good," "righteous," according to norm(s) set forth by heterosexual male standards of sexual-gender morality.

Sexual-gender injustice based in power as a commodity to be possessed is oppression. Oppression is justified by interpreting imbalances in power as givens—sanctioned, meaning ordained by God—and the acts of limiting, injuring, and controlling as atoning sacrifices—necessary to correct, punish, even eradicate sin, meaning anything that is against the will of God. Groups of persons who are the objects of this oppression are presumed to threaten the purity of the community; thus, these groups must be either cleansed and restrained (compelled to act as the controlling group) within or removed from the community. When male clergy enact cleansing and restraint, the practices of oppression are covert—such as preaching and counseling to promote heterosexual patriarchal sexual-gender morality. The practices are covert because they socialize groups to the dominant morality by insisting that they are simply (and rightly) teaching scripture and tradition. Such practices are overt when groups are removed through the establishment of church law that claims to regulate behavior but in effect shuns groups of persons (who they are, not simply what they do). In sum, the role morality of clergy who interpret power as a commodity to be possessed and who enact power as oppression is a morality of sexual-gender injustice—a morality that decides what is due (just) for groups on the basis of an imbalanced (hierarchical, heterosexual, patriarchally privileged) relationship between sexual-gender groups.

In order to transform the role morality of clergy into a morality of sexual-gender justice, power must no longer be interpreted as a commodity. Power must be interpreted as relational, as processes of encounter, and this power must be enacted as sharing rather than possessing. When male clergy acknowledge that the church is a social institution and a human community, wherein norms, habits, and symbols of heterosexual patriarchal morality embed practices of oppression, they take the first step in shifting to an interpretation of power as processes of encounter. The church then becomes a site of encounters that must be disclosed as being processes that may either oppress or liberate. Shifting to an interpretation of power as relational means recognizing that social, cultural, and theological sources are interactively shaping (the practices of) relationships as well as the interpretation of those relationships.

When power is relational, the practice(s) that enacts this power and that will fuel sexual-gender justice is earmarked by courage, partnership, and dialogue. Male clergy who enact power relationally have the courage to confess when they are using scripture and tradition to proof-text sexual-gender oppression and maintain heterosexual patriarchal privilege. In the context of the church that practices relational power, men and women both have the courage to name their complicity in sexual-gender injustice; they release one another from blaming and counterblaming into processes of self-actualization that foster mutuality and interdependency.

Partnership is the indispensable practice of relational power, and partnership recognizes and embraces sexual-gender differences as sources for growth and fulfillment of God's intent for creation. Partnership does not mean that there is always a man and a woman, or a heterosexual person and a homosexual person, paired to do the work of the church. But it does mean that there is always a place (symbolically and physically) through practices of preaching, teaching, counseling, and advocacy that embrace those persons who are potential partners.

Clergy lead the church as a site of sexual-gender justice when their practice(s) of power nurture intentional dialogue. The practices of dialogue entail both face-to-face encounters of talking out the antagonisms between women and men, and the leadership of women *with* men, men *with* women, heterosexual persons *with* homosexual persons in grappling for the meaning of scripture and tradition for the church's life and ministry as faithful witnesses at this time in history. In sum, the role morality of clergy who interpret power as relational and enact power as courage, partnership, and dialogue is the morality of sexual-gender justice—a morality that resists and redresses oppression; reclaims those who have been rejected and removed; and reno-vates[7] through on-going new interpretation of scripture and tradition for the sake of restoring balance to sexual-gender relations. Let us now examine how the understanding of clergy ethics and of sexual-gender ethics proposed in the two sections above cohere.

MINISTERIAL ETHICS

I have defined ministerial ethics as the values and practices of a church's common life, that is, the ethics of the church's life that enables its ministry (its witness) within and outside of its walls. I use ministerial ethics as an overarching category pointing to the interacting ethics of clergy and laity sharing a common life and call to ministry. These interacting ethics are the heart of the church's ability to do ministry and be witnesses. Thus, ministerial ethics may be thought of as the ethics of the church's common good.

When the church gathers in community—to worship, to mourn, to celebrate, to learn, and to deliberate moral, fiscal, governance decisions—the church enacts its ministerial ethics. In this section, I will discuss ministerial ethics as the coalescence of the aforesaid understandings of sexual-gender ethics and clergy ethics that sustain sexual-gender justice. As the ethics of the church's common good with respect to sexual-gender justice, I am concerned with proposing ministerial ethics that understand power as relational and enact power as practices of sexual-gender justice—practices that resist and redress oppression, reclaim those who have been rejected and removed, and continually renovate scripture and tradition for the sake of restoring balance to sexual-gender relations in the church. There are two important questions to be answered in this last section:

(1) What is the theological ethical framework for a ministerial ethics of sexual-gender justice?

(2) How do we ensure that the practices of the church will foster sexual-gender justice?

What is the theological ethical framework for sexual-gender justice? I opened this chapter with a text from the book of Acts and said that that text provides a moral vision for a transformed African American church. The moral vision briefly outlined in the opening paragraphs of this chapter is based in the theological ethical framework that I now present.

The first feature of this theological ethical framework is an understanding of God's power rooted in the Gospel of Luke and "Acts, the Gospel of the Spirit."[8] From the perspective of Luke-Acts, living in relationship with God's power is about living by being led by God's Spirit. Characteristic of God's power is that it is God's Spirit that anoints Jesus for his ministry, and Jesus' mission bears fruit of the Spirit in its ethical mandates of concern for the poor, the captives, the blind, and the oppressed (Luke 4:18; 7:22). Being anointed by the Spirit, Jesus thus announces the reign of God (the power of God) that is fulfilled through him, specifically in the covenant to Abraham to bless all families of the earth and the ability to bear good fruit. One concrete way of bearing good fruit is to love one's enemies (Luke 6:35), and loving enemies is a manifestation of being children of God. Significantly, ethics from a Luke-Acts perspective is "a matter of God's children bearing fruit to the God who promises to bless all families of the earth."[9] A first feature of God's power is that it anoints us to bear fruit as God's children.

Another feature of God's power that follows the first is derived from the book of Acts. The main character of the book of Acts is the Holy Spirit; indeed, it seems that the Spirit "corrects" or even "mocks" at times what the apostles and leaders of the church do and decide. "When read in this manner, the Book of Acts becomes a call to Christians to be open to the action of the Spirit, not only leading them to confront values and practices in society that may need to be subverted, but perhaps even leading them to subvert or question practices and values within the Church itself."[10] In other words, God's power is the activity of the Spirit to subvert or challenge normative expectations that human beings may impose.

Moreover, according to the story of Pentecost, the Spirit gives birth to the church as the fulfillment of Jesus' promise to the disciples. When the Spirit comes at Pentecost, it comes as a "surprising" and "overwhelming" outpouring, and as the disciples receive this outpouring they are confirmed as witnesses to God's deeds of power in the life, death, and resurrection of

Jesus.[11] Accordingly, the church is a community of the Spirit, and this means that its life evidences the work of the Spirit. The earmarks of a community of the Spirit are these: its members (a) live as subjects of God's reign (of peace, justice, equity) in the midst of the present world's reign (that does not recognize God's reign), (b) can communicate with others in their own cultural and linguistic terms, and (c) know that the Spirit destroys privilege (that is, the Spirit is poured out upon "all flesh"—sons and daughters, young and old, male and female).[12]

Furthermore, with this characterization of the book of Acts in mind, the story of Pentecost and the earmarks of the community of the Spirit serve as a reminder to the church that a church that squelches the Spirit is bereft of God's power. So, when does the church squelch the Spirit? The story of Ananias and Sapphira answers this question. The Spirit is squelched when members of the community are not only dishonest by outright lying but also when deceit is the means used to undermine the Spirit's work of destroying privilege. Dishonesty and deceit are obstructions to partnership, the indispensable practice of relational power that must be shared between members of the community. Undermining the Spirit's work of destroying privilege disrupts (if not severs) the connection to God's power as the outpouring of the Spirit that brought the community into being and sustains its life. The practice(s) of hierarchical sexual-gender relations are signs that the church's connection to God's power—the power of the cross, the power of life and love forming a community of unity and mutual service—is threatened.

The theological ethical framework for a ministerial ethics of sexual-gender justice is therefore one grounded in the power of God understood to be the power of the cross and the power of the Spirit. Ministerial ethics of sexual-gender justice thus requires ongoing practices of resocialization. These practices of resocialization are necessary for forming, nurturing, and sustaining the church as a community where its members recognize that all power derives from God and that its life must reflect attempts, not to assert controlling power, but to affirm relations that balance power—women with men, men with women, heterosexual persons with homosexual persons—thus creating sexual-gender justice.

How do we ensure that the practices of the church will foster such sexual-gender justice? Practices are: actions that are indispensable to moral formation; means to a good life; actions intrinsic to a way of life that center, order, and sustain that way of living; and rites that embody what is right. Practices may be formal (sacraments such as baptism or eucharist) or informal (placing doilies on the heads of women) in the church. I contend that practices of the church must be revised, in order to be an effective part of the ongoing resocialization of members. Revising ritual is the means to revising practices. This is the case because one of ritual's gifts is transformation; it assists in the dynamic of social change because "[ritual] is the performance of an act in which people confront one kind of power with another, and rehearse their own future."[13] When new ritual interfaces with practices of the church, those practices become subject to social change as does the community of people who perform the ritual. Also, ritual is important to revising our practices because rituals are often accompanied by stories, and "[ritual and story] are necessary because storytelling and ritualizing together provide the vehicles for reconnecting God's story with our human stories."[14] To illustrate this point about how ritual may revise our practices in the church, I will conclude this chapter with a revision of the practice of eucharist so that it embodies a ministerial ethics of sexual-gender justice.

The practice of eucharist is the rite wherein we remember the death and passion of Jesus as Christ is made present to us in the breaking of bread and the drinking of wine. Important to this practice is the confession and forgiveness of sin, and it is this aspect of the practice that the proposed ritual revision particularly addresses. In most orders of worship, as preparation for taking the wine and bread, we are invited to confess our sins. As stated in the preface to this book, the African American church (like most other churches) has rendered the subject of sexuality and sexual misconduct taboo, and the church is silent about the sexual-gender transgressions committed by and within the life of the church (sins of omission and commission). Thus, the practice of the eucharist can indeed be an appropriate place to begin revising our practices with an eye to sexual-gender justice.

Ordinarily the divine story at the heart of the eucharist is the story of Jesus' passion. In this ritual revision, the central story will be the story of Ananias and Sapphira, the story of community born of Christ's promise of the Spirit broken by the complicity of a man and a woman in dishonesty and deceit that displaces the power of God, the power of the Spirit, the power of life and love, as two members of the community assert the power of privilege and control by withholding that which should be held in common. When the divine story (the biblical story of Ananias and Sapphira) intersects the human story (the story of African American men and women in complicity with sexual-gender injustice in the African American church), the practice of eucharist is revised into a ritual for transforming sexual-gender relations. Importantly, this revision of the practice of eucharist through ritual serves this purpose:

> In our rituals, like our stories, we narrate our existence, that is to say, we individually and collectively express and create a vision of life. Furthermore, through ritual and narrative we mediate the many identities and relationships that shape that life.[15]

A RITUAL REVISION OF THE EUCHARIST

It is a Sunday morning. The choir and congregation are singing "Let us Break Bread Together." The pastor extends an invitation to Holy Communion, and there is the call to confess our sins before God and neighbor. The congregants are instructed to find a woman or man, a boy or girl to face as they recite prayers of confession found on the insert in the bulletin. The instructions and prayers of confession on the bulletin insert read as follows:

Men to Women
If I or any other man has ever done anything to hurt or offend you, and for the manifold transgressions against women, you and every other, I apologize.

Please forgive me and please forgive us.

If you have ever felt demeaned, uncherished, or
your womanhood betrayed in any way;

If I or any other man has failed to see
the light of your sex and the brilliance of your
female spirit, on behalf of all of us, I am
so sorry.

May the beauty of women and the power of
women and the vision of women now burst
forth in our world and our consciousness.

May the mind of man be healed.

May the heart of women repair.

I commit to you and to God that I am, and
shall be, a man who sees your value.

I see your light.

God bless you and your sisters, our mothers
and daughters.

I shall teach my sons to honor you.

May we never go back.

Amen.

Women to Men

If I or any member of my sex has ever done
anything to hurt you or offend you or any
man, please forgive me and please forgive us.

If your life as a man has been stunted or
thwarted by any woman, I now stand in her
stead and apologize for me, for her, for all
womankind.

May God give us a healed vision of what it
means to be a man.

May men receive this healing.

May women receive this healing.

May we see your strength.

May we not emasculate.

May we honor your power and respect your
    mind.

I shall teach my daughters well.

May your past be healed, your future made new
    and strong.

May you reach your fullest joy.

Go, with my love, and the love of all women,
    forever.

Amen.[16]

Words of Christ's forgiveness are spoken. Signs of
peace are exchanged. The Words of Institution are said,
invoking the Holy Spirit to transform the bread and
wine and the people gathered for communion. The ele-
ments are served by passing them among the people,
who commune one another. After all have communed,
the formal prayer of thanksgiving is offered followed by
prayers of thanksgiving spontaneously offered aloud by
any one who has communed. The eucharist service ends
as the community sings, "Let Us Praise God Together."

This ritual revision of the eucharist seeks to reso-
cialize church members by honoring the traditional
practice while at the same time creating dissonance with
the traditional. Honoring the traditional and creating
dissonance are critical to the community's connecting
to the power of God when that connection is threatened by male power as heterosexual patriarchal privilege that seeks to control women and homosexual per-

sons. Ritual revision of the practices of the church is critical to authentic community; for,

> true community begins in the hearts of the people involved. It is not a place of distraction but a place of being. It is not a place where you reform, but a place you go home to. Finding a home is what people in community try to accomplish. In community it is possible to restore a supportive presence for one another, rather than distrust of one another or competitiveness with one another. The others in community are the reason that one feels the way one feels. . . . This interdependency is . . . supportive presence.[17]

Supportive presence is characteristic of authentic community, and transforming the sexual-gender relations in the African American church is surely about restoring the supportive presence of women and men. The African American church must be a place to which women and men, heterosexual and homosexual persons, come home. Our hope for transforming the moral life of the African American church must be built on the willingness of the community's members to sojourn together on a quest for sexual-gender justice.

DIALOGUE THREE
CLERGY AND LAITY—ASKING UNSPEAKABLE QUESTIONS
(A WORKSHOP EXAMINING MINISTERIAL ETHICS)

This workshop pushes us to examine the tensions and metaphors that ground the church's understanding of sexuality and clergy ethics that have rendered such discussions unspeakable in our congregations.

Exploring Tensions

What do you think are the tensions that create sexual-gender injustice and sexual misconduct in the church? Share personal experiences of some of those tensions and examples in the life of the church.

Sexuality

The overarching tension: *passion versus control*

We perceive the tension as: *ecstasy vs. ethics*

Sexuality and spirituality are thus separated from each other.

When we maintain the separation between sexuality and spirituality, we think that sexual-gender injustice and sexual misconduct arise from our *being* sexual creatures rather than from our failure to live ethically as sexual creatures.

We must learn to live between ecstasy and ethics.

The personal challenge: to be aware of the reality of one's own experience, and to behave responsibly.

The church's challenge: to have an honest acknowledgment of our sexual nature (lack of awareness is directly connected with irresponsible acting out of our feelings), and to move away from avoidance of our sexual concerns.

"We can live more faithfully if we consent to live in the tension between two realities: awareness of our feelings and drives and also of the call to behave in responsible ways."[18]

Exploring Tensions

What do you think are the tensions that ground the ethical dilemmas of clergy? Clergy who are present might describe ethical dilemmas that they face.

Authority

The overriding tension: *power vs. vulnerability*

We perceive the tension as: *strength vs. weakness*

This means that clergy subvert their professional or representative power as pastor into personal power, thus abusing legitimate authority.

When clergy abuse their legitimate authority, they forget that the minister is a physical representation of the whole community of faith, of the tradition, of a way of viewing the meaning of life, and—of God.

Clergy must learn to live between power and vulnerability.

The personal challenge: to remember that when you are serving in the role of minister, the exercise of your personal power must always be guided by your professional power.

The church's challenge: to empower its members to exercise their personal power in responding to ministers' abuse of their professional power.[19]

Given these tensions with respect to sexuality and clergy ethics, what metaphors for the church might help us envision living into these tensions, thus creating a healthier moral life in the church?

Do we need new metaphors? Can traditional metaphors for clergy, such as pastor, priest, and prophet, be interpreted to account for the tensions? Can traditional metaphors, such as the body of Christ, the family of God, and the people of God, be interpreted to account for the tensions?

Closure

Write a ritual revision of the practice of baptism that encompasses what you have learned in this workshop.

POSTSCRIPT

This book has used the African American church as a case study for examining sexual-gender ethics, clergy ethics, and ministerial ethics. The important word to all churches from this analysis is that the means for addressing sexual misconduct and sexual-gender injustice as well as for developing an adequate sexual ethic will not be the formulation of codes of conduct alone. The churches must transform their moral life (values and practices) if the church is to be a site of sexual-gender justice, a place of God's power—a community of the Spirit.

In this postscript, I would now like to say a few additional words about why I wrote the book as I have done so and comment on what may seem to some to be glaring omissions in my argument. I wrote this book to speak to clergy, lay people, and seminarians as my primary audience. If graduate students and academic Christian ethicists find its contents helpful to theorizing about sex, sexuality, gender, sexual orientation, and similar issues in the life of the church, then I will be pleased. But I will also not be disappointed if these two groups feel that I should have spent more time on reviewing academic literature and formulating a constructive Christian sexual ethic.

I decided to use theoretical categories from contemporary Christian ethics discussions and social construction gender theory to accomplish the task of descriptive ethical analysis, thus I have only engaged various insights of those theories that are most helpful to such descriptive disclosure. However, I have tried not to allow theory to overwhelm the aim of giving clergy, lay people, and seminarians some guidance as to what's at stake, and for whom, in the quest to transform the moral life of the church with respect to sexual-gender injustice. Therefore, the use of poignant quotations as epigraphs to open chapters as well as scenarios with questions followed by dialogues is an intentional ethical methodological strategy on my part to engage the reader by provoking her or his moral imagination using these various "ethical stimuli." If a clergy person, lay person, and/or seminarian takes this book to heart and uses it as a kind of handbook for retreats, book discussion groups, and/or for personal introspective examination of his or her ministry and the ministerial ethics of the church, I will have truly done what I set out to do.

Now, to the matter of what may seem to be glaring omissions in my argument. I will point to three. First, why didn't I speak directly to what the Bible has to say about sexuality, sex, and sexual orientation? My immediate answer is this: I do not think that our "fights" in the church about sexuality, sex, and sexual orientation are at their deepest roots about the interpretation of biblical texts. Rather, the deep roots of these fights can be found in our fears of losing control of the institutions of the church that have offered us security from what we in the church have sometimes characterized (and still often do) as the moral decadence of the culture. The deep roots are to be found in our fears of that which we do not understand about persons who are different, who are what we have been socialized to think of not only as "deviant" from what is "normal" but also as "morally depraved."

There are many good texts out there already that contain important new exegetical insights about those traditional scriptural texts that are used to support arguments for the subordination of women and against homosexuality. Among the excellent texts cited in my bibliography that do this exegetical work are the books or articles by Danna Nolan Fewell and Davis M. Gunn (*Gender, Power & Promise*), Clarice Martin ("The *Haustafeln* (Household Codes) in African American Biblical Interpretation"), and Patricia Beattie Jung and Ralph E. Smith (*Heterosexism: An Ethical Challenge*). It has been my experience, however, that even such careful and scholarly exegetical reinterpretation of those traditional texts is not effective in engendering the kind of dialogue that I seek to invite by the method and content of the argument that I use in this book.

123

Furthermore, it is clear to me that only a certain spectrum of the churches (liberally inclined already on other matters of injustice) is willing to engage the revisionist biblical scholarship. Yet, I do think that any church—from conservative Pentecostals/neo-Pentecostals to evangelical moderate Baptists to Full Gospelers to liberal centrist Baptists, Presbyterians, Methodists, or Episcopalians to New Thought Christian traditions—can and should be engaged in uncovering the social myths that constrain our relationships as women and men, and that consequently deny the power of God's power to direct the life of the church (even if we don't understand where God's going with all of this). What I think the Bible contributes to the conversation about sexuality, sex, and sexual orientation is a conversation about whose church it is anyway (God's) and a reminder that within the biblical witness there is always surprise and disruption of life as usual when we look at what God is doing, how Jesus is ministering, and when the faithful truly "let go and let God." Uncovering what is going in our relationships with one another as human beings is a critical first step in preparation for reengaging the biblical text so as to listen for a new word from God about who we are to be and what we are to do as sexual beings.

Related to the question of why I do not address the Bible directly on traditional texts is the second area that I think that some will see as an omission on my part. This second omission is my apparent failure to give concrete, or at least particular, guidelines for sexual-gender morality and clergy ethics. Again, there are numerous very good books already in print setting forth guidelines and constructive theological proposals for an improved sexual morality. In the bibliography, texts by Marie Fortune (*Love Does No Harm*), Christine Gudorf (*Body, Sex, and Pleasure*), Marvin Ellison (*Erotic Justice*) Karen LeBacqz and Ronald G. Barton (*Sex in the Parish*), and Kelly Brown Douglas (*Sexuality and the Black Church*) are significant examples.

Also, some may perceive my failure to posit specific guidelines as my captivity to cultural norms of relativism. That, however, is not the case. Although I do think that morality is socially embedded and constructed and is not an entity out there to be found in texts (even sacred ones) or traditions, I think that morality is to be discerned as it functions in life because of the interpretations of values and norms that we derive from sacred texts and traditions. Thus, that which is moral is relative to a specific historical time, locale, context, and community, but it is not a relativistic enterprise. On matters pertaining to sexuality, sex, and sexual orientation, the church can not abdicate its responsibility to do the hard work of engaging the sacred text and traditions of the faith for the meaning that such will provide for life in the twenty-first century church and society. We in the church must not be gatekeepers of the Bible or traditions in such a way that they become stagnant, thus rendering them relics to be treasured and protected but not a "lamp unto our feet" that will and can guide us down the unknown paths of moral life in a new millennium. If we clutch the Bible and our traditions so tightly that they no longer have the power to reveal God to us, then we will have to ask ourselves whether we really know anything about the first commandment. The Bible and our traditions become idols when we worship them rather than God.

Lastly, there are those who, perhaps, think that I do not have an accurate read on the pulse of the churches. I have now been teaching in theological schools and seminaries for fifteen years, and I have been in ordained ministry for seventeen years. I know that these credentials do not give me special insight or understanding. However, these credentials do squarely place me in the trenches with church folk, and I can respond only to what I hear. And I hear women and men speaking out in frustration and pain as well as hope to a desire to be reconciled in the churches, "to make the wounded whole." Thus, I prayerfully have sought and am seeking God's Word to us (all of us) as to healing and the way to wholeness. This book is just one answer that I have received from God while on my prayer quest.

ENDNOTES

Preface

1. My decision to use a hyphenated term, sexual-gender ethics, derives from my reading of Candace West and Don H. Zimmerman, "Doing Gender," in *The Social Construction of Gender,* ed. Judith Lorber and Susan A. Farrell (Newbury Park, CA: Sage Publications, 1991), 13–34; and Patricia Hill Collins, *Black Feminist Thought: Knowledge, Consciousness, and the Politics of Empowerment* (New York: Routledge, 1991), chap. 8. A full explanation of the term will be given in chapter 1 of this book.

2. Ruth E. Igoe, "$6 Million Award in Harassment Case," *The Kansas City Star,* 4 December 1999.

3. Jualynne E. Dodson, *Engendering Church: Women, Power, and the AME Church* (Lanham, MD: Rowman & Littlefield Publishers, 2002), 1.

4. Alice Walker, *In Search of Our Mothers' Gardens* (New York: Harcourt, Brace, Jovanovich, 1983), xi–xii. The term womanist was coined by Alice Walker, and many black women religious scholars have adopted the term as signifier for the fact that our theological reflection takes seriously black women's relgious experience, cultural life, and socioeconomic and political realities.

CHAPTER ONE

1. C. Eric Lincoln and Lawrence H. Mamiya, *The Black Church in the African American Experience* (Durham, NC: Duke University Press, 1990), 1, lists these seven major black denominations: the African Methodist Episcopal (AME) Church; the African Methodist Episcopal Zion (AMEZ) Church; the Christian Methodist Episcopal (CME) Church; the National Baptist Convention, U.S.A., Incorporated (NBC); the National Baptist Convention of America, Unincorporated (NBCA); the Progressive National Baptist Convention (PNBC); and the Church of God in Christ (COGIC). Lincoln and Mamiya's study is concerned only with "the independent, historic, and totally black controlled denominations, which were founded after the Free African Society of 1787 and which constituted the core of black Christians." I am, however, including African American congregations within white denominations whenever the clerical leadership and the majority of the membership is African American, because this analysis is concerned with African Americans who share a social, political, and economic history that generates common experiences out of which they construct and act out a distinctive sexual-gender morality in whatever context.

2. Ibid.

3. For elaboration of this point see chapter 1, "A Sociology of Black Liberation," in my book, *Awake, Arise & Act: A Womanist Call for Black Liberation* (Cleveland: Pilgrim Press, 1994).

4. Beth E. Vanfossen, *The Structure of Social Inequality* (Boston: Little and Brown, 1979), and James M. Gustafson, *Treasure in Earthen Vessels: The Church as a Human Community* (Chicago: University of Chicago Press, 1961), inform my discussion at this point.

5. Larry L. Rasmussen, *Moral Fragments and Moral Community: A Proposal for Church in Society* (Minneapolis: Fortress Press, 1993), 154–56, 160–61.

6. The last part of this definition is taken from Iris Marion Young, *Justice and the Politics of Difference* (Princeton, NJ: Princeton University Press, 1990), 41.

7. Arthur Brittan and Mary Maynard, *Sexism, Racism and Oppression* (New York: Basil Blackwell, 1984), 213.

8. Elizabeth Janeway, *Powers of the Weak* (New York: Alfred A. Knopf, 1980), 3.

9. Judith L. Orr, "Hard Work, Hard Lovin,' Hard Times, Hardly Worth It: Care of Working-Class Men," in *The Care of Men,* ed. Christie Cozad Neuger and James Newton Poling (Nashville: Abingdon Press, 1997), 74.

10. Ibid., 74–75.

11. Christine E. Gudorf, "The Social Construction of Sexuality: Implications for the Churches," in *God Forbid: Religion and Sex in American Public Life,* ed. Kathleen M. Sands (New York: Oxford University Press, 2000), 47.

12. Ibid., 49–52.

13. Ibid., 53.

14. Elizabeth Janeway, *Man's World, Woman's Place: A Study in Social Mythology* (New York: William Morrow, 1971), 295–96.

CHAPTER TWO

1. Donna L. Franklin, *What's Love Got To Do with It?: Understanding and Healing the Rift between Black Men and Women* (New York: Simon & Schuster, 2000), 212.

2. Manning Marable, "The Black Male: Searching Beyond Stereotypes," in *The American Black Male: His*

Present Status and His Future, ed. Richard G. Majors and Jacob U. Gordon (Chicago: Nelson-Hall Publishers, 1994), 70.

3. Franklin, chap. 2.

4. Ibid., 37.

5. Ibid., 51–52.

6. This social mythology derives from my reading of works such as Michelle Wallace's *Black Macho and the Myth of the Superwoman* (New York: Dial Press, 1979); bell hooks' *Ain't I a Woman: Black Women and Feminism* (Boston: South End Press, 1981); and Patricia Hill-Collins' *Black Feminist Thought: Knowledge, Consciousness, and the Politics of Empowerment* (New York: Routledge, 1991).

7. See Paula Giddings, *When and Where I Enter: The Impact of Black Women on Race and Sex in America* (New York: Bantam Books, 1985), chap. 18, for a discussion that supports this analysis.

8. bell hooks, *killing race: ending racism* (New York: Henry Holt, 1995), 66. Cf. Clyde W. Franklin II, "Ain't I a Man? The Efficacy of Black Masculinities for Men's Studies in the 1990s," in *The American Black Male: His Present Status and His Future,* ed. Richard G. Majors and Jacob U. Gordon (Chicago: Nelson-Hall Publishers, 1994), 277–78.

9. Cornel West, *Race Matters* (Boston: Beacon Press, 1993), 83.

10. Gail Elizabeth Wyatt, *Stolen Women: Reclaiming Our Sexuality, Taking Back Our Lives* (New York: John Wiley & Sons, 1997), 4.

11. Ibid., 10–20. Wyatt is careful not to romanticize African traditional rites of passage for females, especially noting the dangerous practice of female circumscion.

12. Ibid., 20–22.

13. Ibid., 31–37.

14. Ibid., 36–38. Examples of statements on the survey per each stereotype: The Mammy—"Some women have large buttocks and legs. The Workhorse—Some women think that sex is to have babies and not for enjoyment. The She-devil—Some women use sex to get what they want. Some women have babies to receive financial support like welfare."

15. Ibid., 71–74.

16. Clyde W. Franklin II, "Men's Studies, the Men's Movement, and the Study of Black Masculinities: Further Demystification of Masculinities in America," in *The American Black Male: His Present Status and His Future*, ed. Richard G. Majors and Jacob U. Gordon (Chicago: Nelson-Hall Publishers, 1994), 5.

17. Ibid., 11.

18. Ibid., 12–13, 14.

19. Ibid., 15–19.

20. Clyde W. Franklin II, "Ain't I a Man?" in *The American Black Male*, 276, 277.

21. Ibid., 280–82.

22. See Elizabeth V. Spelman, "'Race' and the Labor of Identity," in *Racism and Philosophy*, ed. Susan E. Babbitt and Sue Campbell (Ithaca, NY: Cornell University Press, 1999), 210–11, for a full explication of this concept.

23. "Statement of Professor Anita F. Hill to the Senate Judiciary Committee, October 11, 1991," in *Court of Appeal: The Black Community Speaks Out on the Racial and Sexual Politics of Thomas Vs. Hill*, ed. Robert Chrisman and Robert L. Allen (New York: Ballantine Books, 1992), 21.

24. "Statement of Judge Clarence Thomas to the Senate Judiciary Committee, October 11, 1991," in *Court of Appeal*, 13.

25. "Second Statement from Judge Clarence Thomas, October 11, 1991," in *Court of Appeal*, 22.

26. Jacquelyne Johnson Jackson, "'Them Against Us': Anita Hill v. Clarence Thomas" in *Court of Appeal,* 99–105, is a representative essay of this point of view.

27. Rev. Joseph E. Lowery, "The SCLC Position: Confirm Clarence Thomas," in *Court of Appeal,* 283–85.

28. Toni Morrison, "Introduction: Friday on the Potomac" in *Race-ing, Justice, En-gendering Power: Essays on Anita Hill, Clarence Thomas and the Construction of Social Reality* (New York: Pantheon Books, 1992), xvi–xvii.

CHAPTER THREE

1. Emilie M. Townes, "Keeping a Clean House Will Not Keep a Man at Home: An Unctuous Womanist Rhetoric of Justice," in *New Visions for the Americas: Religious Engagement and Social Transformation* (Minneapolis: Fortress Press, 1993), 141.

2. James H. Cone, *For My People: Black Theology and the Black Church (Where have we been and where are we going?)* (Maryknoll, NY: Orbis Books, 1984), 137.

3. Linda Faye Williams, "Power and Gender: A Glass Ceiling Limits the Role of Black Women in the Civil Rights Community," *Emerge* (December/January 1995), 63–65.

4. Michael Eric Dyson, "When You Divide Body and Soul, Problems Multiply: The Black Church and Sex," in *Race Rules: Navigating the Color Line* (New York: Addison-Wesley, 1996), 78–80, 81–82.

5. E. Franklin Frazier, *The Negro Church in America* (New York: Schocken Books, 1974), chap. 3. The book was first published in the United States in 1964.

6. C. Eric Lincoln, *The Black Church Since Frazier* (New York: Schocken Books, 1974), 107.

7. Ibid., 109–10.

8. The term is borrowed from Peter J. Paris, *The Social Teaching of the Black Churches* (Philadelphia: Fortress Press, 1985), chap. 1.

9. Cf. Peter J. Paris, *The Spirituality of African Peoples: The Search for a Common Moral Discourse* (Minneapolis: Fortress Press, 1995), 96–97. Paris describes the pastor's role as analogous to that of the patriarch in the traditional African family and royalty in the tribal community.

10. Cheryl Townsend Gilkes, "The Role of Church and Community Mothers: Ambivalent American Sexism or Fragmented African Familyhood?" in *"If It Wasn't for the Women . . .": Black Women's Experience and Womanist Culture in Church and Community* (Maryknoll, NY: Orbis Books, 2001), 61–75.

11. Cheryl Townsend Gilkes, "The Politics of 'Silence': Dual-Sex Political Systems and Women's Traditions of Conflict," in *"If It Wasn't for the Women,* 92–117.

12. See Gilkes, "The Politics of 'Silence,'" 109–12, for examples of this tradition of biblical feminism as found in the writings of Maria Stewart, Sojourner Truth, and Virginia Broughton and the creation of a book of names for unnamed women in the Bible by women in the Church of God in Christ.

13. Ibid., 114–15. Nannie Helen Burroughs was the church woman with whom the idea for a national observance of Women's Day in the Baptist church originated. Burroughs' vision for Women's Day was that it would be a time for "raising women" and not simply raising money for missions. The observance spread from the Baptists to other black denominations.

14. Ibid., 74.

15. Prathia Hall Wynn, "Becoming Sisters and Brothers in Struggle" (a lecture at the Kelly Miller Smith Institute, Vanderbilt Divinity School Conference, "What Does It Mean to be Black and Christian?" October 1991) as quoted in William H. Meyers, *God's Yes Was Louder Than My No: Rethinking the African American Call to Ministry* (Grand Rapids, MI: William B. Eerdmans, 1994), 227–28.

16. I am indebted to the discussion of moral corruption found in Stephen L. Carter, *(integrity)* (New York: Basic Books, 1996), 12–14.

17. The term, "sexualized behavior" is found in the training curriculum entitled "Clergy Misconduct: Sexual Abuse in the Ministerial Relationship" produced by the Center for the Prevention of Sexual and Domestic Violence in Seattle, Washington. Sexualized behavior refers to ways of being and doing that draw attention to or make overt the sexual dimension of human behavior.

18. Victor Anderson, *Beyond Ontological Blackness: An Essay on African American Religious and Cultural Criticism* (New York: Continuum Publishing, 1995), 22, 38. Anderson notes that "cultural criticism can be both descriptive (insofar as it describes human activities) and constructive (insofar as it commends human activities worthy of pursuing in the interest of cultural fulfillment)," and "its two defining aspects [are] social analysis and the critique of ideology." "Religious criticism is a form of cultural criticism and therefore a culturally descriptive and constructive activity;" "as a viable mode of cultural criticism, religious criticism can be enlightening and iconoclastic when it exposes and rejects totalities (race, class, gender, and sexuality) that would deny the cultural fulfillment of persons on the grounds of their differences—whether ethnicity social status, biological determinants, or sexual orientation."

CHAPTER FOUR

1. Sally Purvis, *The Power of the Cross: Foundations for a Christian Feminist Ethic of Community* (Nashville: Abingdon Press, 1993), 73–78.

2. Ibid., 70–72.

3. Stephen Carter, *(integrity)* (New York: Basic Books, 1996), 10.

4. Ibid., 10–12.

5. Ibid., 28.

6. I am not unaware of discussions of codes as ethics of character such as found in Karen Lebacqz, *Professional Ethics: Power and Paradox* (Nashville,: Abingdon Press, 1985); Stanley Hauerwas, "Clerical Character: Reflecting on Ministerial Morality," *Word and World* 6/2 (1991): 181–93; and selected essays in James P. Wind, Russell Burck, Paul F. Camenisch, and Dennis P. McCann, eds., *Clergy Ethics in a Changing Society: Mapping the Terrain* (Louisville: Westminster John Knox Press, 1991). However, I think that the codes of ethics actually adopted and instituted by denominations serve a regulatory function and not one of character formation. My decision not to focus on codes in this discussion may also be seen as aligning with a feminist interpretation of a New Testament perspective on sexual ethics; "the New Testament certainly warns against the moral security and even self-righteousness which can accompany the elaboration of behavioral codes, even as it calls us, in a context of responsibility to the good of the whole community, to a very high moral standard of loving 'the neighbor' (and enemy) as ourselves." Mary McClintock Fulkerson, "Church Documents on Human Sexuality and the Authority of Scripture," *Interpretation* 59/1 (January 1995): 15.

7. These terms of justice are borrowed from Karen Lebacqz, *Justice in an Unjust World: Foundations for a*

Christian Approach to Justice (Minneapolis: Augsburg Publishing, 1987).

8. I am borrowing from Justo L. Gonzalez, *Acts: The Gospel of the Spirit* (Maryknoll, NY: Orbis Books, 2001).

9. This part of the discussion is indebted to Robert L. Brawley, "The Power of God at Work in the Children of God," in *Biblical Ethics & Homosexuality: Listening to Scripture* (Louisville: Westminster John Knox Press, 1996), 41–42.

10. Gonzalez, *Acts: The Gospel of the Spirit*, 8.

11. Ibid., 13–26.

12. Ibid., 43–48.

13. Tom F. Driver, *Liberating Rites: Understanding the Transformative Power of Ritual* (Boulder, CO: Westview Press, 1998), 167, 188.

14. Herbert Anderson and Edward Foley, *Mighty Stories, Dangerous Rituals: Weaving Together the Human and the Divine* (San Francisco: Jossey-Bass Publishers, 1998), ix.

15. Ibid., 26.

16. Marianne Williamson, *Illuminata: Thoughts, Prayers, Rites of Passage* (New York: Random House, 1994), 231–32.

17. Malidoma Patrice Some, *Ritual: Power, Healing, and Community* (New York: Penguin Books, 1993), 51.

18. This section of the workshop is based on my reading of Celia Allison Hahn, *Sexual Paradox: Creative Tensions in Our Lives and in Our Congregations* (Cleveland: Pilgrim Press, 1991).

19. This section of the workshop is based on my reading of Karen Lebacqz, *Professional Ethics: Power and Paradox* (Nashville: Abingdon Press, 1985).

BIBLIOGRAPHY

Acker, Joan. "Hierarchies, Jobs, Bodies: A Theory of Gendered Organizations." In *The Social Construction of Gender*, ed. Judith Lorber and Susan A. Farrell. Newbury, CA: Sage Publications, 1991.

Anderson, Herbert, and Edward Foley. *Mighty Stories, Dangerous Rituals: Weaving Together the Human and the Divine*. San Francisco: Jossey-Bass Publishers, 1998.

Anderson, Victor. *Beyond Ontological Blackness: An Essay on African American Religious and Cultural Criticism*. New York: Continuum Publishing, 1995.

Baker-Fletcher, Garth Kasimu. *Xodus: An African American Male Journey*. Minneapolis: Fortress Press, 1996.

Baker-Fletcher, Karen, and Garth Kasimu. *My Sister, My Brother: Womanist and Xodus God-Talk*. Maryknoll, NY: Orbis Books, 1997.

Bell, Catherine. *Ritual Theory, Ritual Practice*. New York: Oxford University Press, 1992.

Billingsley, Andrew. *Black Families in White America*. New York: Simon & Schuster, 1968.

Brawley, Robert L., ed. *Biblical Ethics & Homosexuality: Listening to Scripture*. Louisville: Westminster John Knox Press, 1996.

Brittan, Arthur, and Mary Maynard. *Sexism, Racism, and Oppression.* New York,: Blackwell, 1984.

Burrell, Sherrill. "Improving and Strengthening Black Male-Female Relationships." In *The Black Family: Past, Present, & Future,* ed. Lee N. June. Grand Rapids, MI: Zondervan Publishing, 1991.

Cahill, Lisa Sowle. *Sex, Gender & Chrisitian Ethics.* New York: Cambridge University Press, 1996.

_____. *Between the Sexes: Foundations for a Christian Ethics of Sexuality.* Philadelphia: Fortress Press, 1985.

Cannon, Katie G. *Black Womanist Ethics.* Atlanta: Scholars Press, 1988.

_____. *Katie's Canon: Womanism and the Soul of the Black Community.* New York: Continuum Publishing, 1995.

Capps, Donald. "Sex in the Parish: Social Scientific Explanations for Why It Occurs." *The Journal of Pastoral Care.* 47/4 (winter 1993).

Carter, Stephen L. *(integrity).* New York: Basic Books, 1996.

Cherry, Kittredge, and Zalmon Sherwood. *Equal Rites: Lesbian and Gay Worship Ceremonies, and Celebrations.* Louisville: Westminster John Knox Press, 1995.

Chrisman, Robert, and Robert L. Allen. *Court of Appeal: The Black Community Speaks Out on The Racial and Sexual Politics of Thomas vs. Hill.* New York: Ballantine Books, 1992.

Collins, Patricia Hill. *Black Feminist Thought: Knowledge, Consciousness, and the Politics of Empowerment.* New York: Routledge, 1991.

Cone, James H. *For My People: Black Theology and the Black Church.* Maryknoll, NY: Orbis Books, 1984.

Cooper-Lewter, Nicholas, and Henry H. Mitchell. *Soul Theology: The Heart of American Black Culture.* Nashville: Abingdon Press, 1986.

Davies, Susan E. "Reflections on the Theological Roots of Abusive Behavior." In *Redefining Sexual Ethics: A Sourcebook of Essays, Stories, and Poems,* ed. Susan E. Davies and Eleanor H. Haney. Cleveland: Pilgrim Press, 1991.

Dawsey, Darrell. *Living to Tell About It: Young Black Men in America Speak Their Piece.* New York: Anchor Books, 1996.

D'Angelo, Mary Rose. "Women in Luke-Acts: A Redactional View." *Journal of Biblical Literature* 109/3 (1990): 441–61.

Dodson, Jualynne E. *Engendering Church: Women, Power, and the AME Church.* Lanham, MD: Rowman & Littlefield Publishers, 2002.

Douglas, Kelly Brown. *The Black Christ.* Maryknoll, NY: Orbis Books, 1994.

———. *Sexuality and the Black Church: A Womanist Perspective.* Maryknoll, NY: Orbis Books, 1999.

Driver, Tom F. *Liberating Rites: Understanding the Transformative Power of Ritual.* Boulder, CO: Westview Press, 1998.

Duck, Ruth C. *Gender and the Name of God.* New York: Pilgrim Press, 1991.

Dyson, Michael Eric. "Sex, Race, and Class." In *Reflecting Black: African American Cultural Criticism.* Minneapolis: University of Minnesota Press, 1993.

———. "When You Divide Body and Soul, Problems Multiply: The Black Church and Sex" in *Race Rules: Navigating the Color Line.* Reading, MA: Addison-Wesley, 1996.

Ellison, Marvin M. *Erotic Justice: A Liberating Ethic of Sexuality.* Louisville: Westminster John Knox Press, 1996.

———. "Refusing to Be 'Good Soldiers': An Agenda for Men." In *Redefining Sexual Ethics: A Sourcebook of Essays, Stories, and Poems,* ed. Susan E. Davies and Eleanor H. Haney. Cleveland: Pilgrim Press, 1991.

Eugene, Toinette. "While Love is Unfashionable: Ethical Implications of Black Spirituality and Sexuality." In *Women's Consciousness, Women's Conscience,* ed. Barbara Hikert Andolsen, Christine Gudorf, and Mary D. Pellauer. Minneapolis: Winston Press, 1985. Reprint San Francisco: Harper & Row, 1987.

_____. "The Shaman Says . . . Womanist Reflection on Pastoral Care of African American Men." In *The Care of Men.* Nashville: Abingdon Press, 1997.

Evans, James H. *We Have Been Believers: An African American Systematic Theology.* Minneapolis: Fortress Press, 1992.

Farajaje-Jones, Elias. "Breaking Silence: Toward an In-the-Life Theology." In *Black Theology: A Documentary History, Volume Two: 1980–1992,* ed. James H. Cone and Gayraud S. Wilmore. Maryknoll, NY: Orbis Books, 1993.

Fewell, Danna Nolan, and David M. Gunn. *Gender, Power & Promise: The Subject of the Bible's First Story.* Nashville: Abingdon Press, 1993.

Fortune, Marie M. *Love Does No Harm: Sexual Ethics for the Rest of Us.* New York: Continuum Publishing, 1995.

Franklin, Clyde W. II. "Ain't I a Man? The Efficacy of Black Masculinities for Men's Studies in the 1990s" and "Men's Studies, the Men's Movement, and the Study of Black Masculinities: Further Demystification of Masculinities in America." In *The American Black Male: His Present Status and His Future,* ed. Richard G. Majors and Jacob U. Gordon. Chicago: Nelson-Hall Publishers, 1994.

Franklin, Donna L. *What's Love Got to Do With It?: Understanding and Healing the Rift Between Black Men and Women.* New York: Simon & Schuster, 2000.

Franklin, Robert Michael. "The Safest Place on Earth: The Culture of Black Congregations." In *American Congregations: Volume 2: New Perspectives in the Study of Congrega-*

tions, ed. James P. Wind and James W. Lewis. Chicago: University of Chicago Press, 1994.

———. *Another's Day's Journey: Black Churches Confronting the American Crisis.* Minneapolis: Fortress Press, 1997.

Frazier, E. Franklin. *The Negro Church in America.* New York: Schocken Books, 1974.

Fulkerson, Mary McClintock. "Church Documents on Human Sexuality and the Authority of Scripture." *Interpretation* 48/1 (January 1995): 5–16.

Giddings, Paula. *When and Where I Enter: The Impact of Black Women on Race and Sex in America.* New York: Bantam Books, 1984.

Gilkes, Cheryl Townsend. "The Roles of Church and Community Mothers: Ambivalent American Sexism or Fragmented African Familyhood?" *Journal of Feminist Studies in Religion* 2/1 (spring 1986).

———. "'Plenty Good Room . . .' In a Changing Black Church." In *One Nation Under God?: Religion and American Culture,* ed. Marjorie Garber and Rebecca L. Walkowitz. New York: Routledge, 1999.

———. *"If It Wasn't for the Women . . .": Black Women's Experience and Womanist Culture in Church and Community.* Maryknoll, NY: Orbis Books, 2001.

Gilson, Anne Bathurst. *Eros Breaking Free: Interpreting Sexual Theo-Ethics.* Cleveland: Pilgrim Press, 1995.

Gomes, Peter J. *The Good Book: Reading the Bible With Mind and Heart.* New York: William Morrow, 1996.

Gonzalez, Justo L. *Acts: The Gospel of the Spirit.* Maryknoll, NY: Orbis Books, 2001.

Grant, Jacquelyn. *White Women's Christ, Black Women's Jesus: Feminist Christology and Womanist Response.* Atlanta: Scholars Press, 1989.

Gudorf, Christine E. *Victimization: Examining Christian Complicity.* Philadelphia: Trinity Press International, 1992.

_____. "The Social Construction of Sexuality: Implications for the Churches." In *God Forbid: Religion and Sex in American Public Life,* ed. Kathleen M. Sands. New York: Oxford University Press, 2000.

_____. *Body, Sex, and Pleasure: Reconstructing Christian Sexual Ethics.* Cleveland: Pilgrim Press, 1994.

Gustafson, James M. *Treasure in Earthen Vessels: The Church as a Human Community.* Chicago,: University of Chicago Press, 1961.

Hahn, Celia Allison. *Sexual Paradox: Creative Tensions in Our Lives and in Our Congregations.* Cleveland: Pilgrim Press, 1991.

Hardman-Cromwell, Youtha C. "Power and Sexual Abuse in Ministry." *Journal of Religion.* 38/1 (1981).

Hernton, Calvin C. *Sex and Racism in America.* New York: Anchor Books, 1965.

Heyward, Carter. "Heterosexism: Enforcing Male Supremacy." In *Redefining Sexual Ethics: A Sourcebook of Essays, Stories, and Poems,* ed. Susan E. Davies and Eleanor H. Haney. Cleveland: Pilgrim Press, 1991.

Hill, Renee. "Who Are We for Each Other?: Sexism, Sexuality and Womanist Theology." In *Black Theology: A Documentary History, Volume Two: 1980–1992,* ed. James H. Cone and Gayraud S. Wilmore. Maryknoll, NY: Orbis Books, 1993.

hooks, bell. *Ain't I A Woman: Black Women and Feminism.* Boston: South End Press, 1981.

_____. "Reflections on Race and Sex." In *Yearning: Race, Gender, and Cultural Politics.* Boston: South End Press, 1990.

_____. "Challenging Sexism in Black Life" in *Killing Rage, Ending Racism.* New York: Henry Holt, 1995.

hooks, bell, and Cornel West. *Breaking Bread: Insurgent Black Intellectual Life.* Boston: South End Press, 1991.

Hutchinson, Earl Ofari. *The Assassination of the Black Male Image*. New York: Simon & Schuster, 1994, 1996.

Igoe, Ruth E. "$6 Million Award in Harassment Case; Former Pastor Said Problems Had Gone on for Years." *The Kansas City Star.* 4 December 1999.

Janeway, Elizabeth. *Man's World, Woman's Place: A Study in Social Mythology*. New York: William Morrow, 1971.

_____. *Powers of the Weak*. New York: Alfred A. Knopf, 1980.

June, Lee N., editor. *Men to Men: Perspectives of Sixteen African-American Christian Men*. Grand Rapids, MI: Zondervan Publishing, 1996.

_____. *The Black Family: Past, Present & Future: Perspectives of Sixteen Black Christian Leaders*. Grand Rapids, MI: Zondervan Publishing, 1991.

Jung, Patricia Beattie, and Ralph E. Smith. *Heterosexism: An Ethical Challenge*. Albany, NY: State University of New York Press, 1993.

Kantor, Martin. *Homophobia: Description, Development, & Dynamics of Gay Bashing*. Westport, CT: Praeger, 1998.

Lebacqz, Karen, and Ronald G. Barton. *Sex in the Parish*. Louisville, KY: Westminster John Knox Press, 1991.

Lebacqz, Karen. *Professional Ethics: Power and Paradox*. Nashville: Abingdon Press, 1985.

_____. *Justice in an Unjust World: Foundations for a Christian Approach to Justice*. Minneapolis: Augsburg Publishing, 1987.

Lincoln, C. Eric. *The Black Church Since Frazier*. New York: Schocken Books, 1974.

Lincoln, C. Eric, and Lawrence H. Mamiya. *The Black Church in the African American Experience*. Durham, NC: Duke University Press, 1990.

Marable, Manning. "The Black Male: Searching Beyond Stereotypes." In *The American Black Male: His Present Status and His Future,* ed. Richard G. Majors and Jacob U. Gordon. Chicago: Nelson-Hall Publishers, 1994.

Martin, Clarice J. "The *Haustafeln* (Household Codes) in African American Biblical Interpretation: 'Free Slaves' and 'Subordinate Women.'" In *Stony the Road We Trod: African American Biblical Interpretation*. Minneapolis: Fortress Press, 1991.

Matthews, Donald H. "Love and Work Among African American Men." In *The Care of Men*, ed. Christie Cozad Neuger and James Newton Poling. Nashville: Abingdon Press, 1997.

McKenzie, Vashti M. *Not Without a Struggle: Leadership Development for African American Women in Ministry*. Cleveland: United Church Press, 1996.

Millner, Denene and Nick Chiles. *What Brothers Think, What Sistahs Know: The Real Deal on Love and Relationships*. New York: William Morrow, 1999.

Morey, Ann-Janine. "Blaming Women for the Sexually Abusive Male Pastor." *The Christian Century*, 5 October 1988.

Morrison, Toni, ed. *Race-ing, Justice, En-gendering Power: Essays on Anita Hill, Clarence Thomas, and the Construction of Social Reality*. New York: Pantheon Books, 1992.

Myers, William H. *God's Yes Was Louder Than My No: Rethinking the African American Call to Ministry*. Grand Rapids, MI: William B. Eerdmans, 1994.

Nelson, James B. *Between Two Gardens: Reflections on Sexuality and Religious Experience*. New York: Pilgrim Press, 1983.

———. *Embodiment: An Approach to Sexuality and Christian Theology*. Minneapolis: Augsburg Publishing, 1978.

———. "Embracing Masculinity." In *Redefining Sexual Ethics: A Sourcebook of Essays, Stories, and Poems*, ed. Susan E. Davies and Eleanor H. Haney. Cleveland: Pilgrim Press, 1991.

Neuger, Christine Cozad, and James Newton Poling. "Gender and Theology." In *The Care of Men*. Nashville: Abingdon Press, 1997.

O'Day, Gail R. "Acts." In *The Women's Bible Commentary*, ed. Carol A. Newsom and Sharon H. Ringe. Louisville: Westminster John Knox Press, 1992.

Orr, Judith L. "Hard Work, Hard Lovin,' Hard Times, Hardly Worth It: Care of Working-Class Men." In *The Care of Men*, ed. Christie Cozad Neuger and James Newton Poling. Nashville: Abingdon Press, 1997.

Paris, Peter. *The Social Teaching of the Black Churches*. Philadelphia,: Fortress Press, 1989.

_____. *The Spirituality of African Peoples: The Search for A Common Moral Discourse*. Minneapolis: Fortress Press, 1995.

Patterson, Sheron C. *New Faith: A Black Christian Woman's Guide to Reformation, Re-Creation, Rediscovery, Renaissance, Resurrection, and Revival*. Minneapolis: Fortress Press, 2000.

Pellauer, Mary. "Sex, Power, and the Family of God." *Christianity and Crisis*, 16 February 1987.

Pharr, Suzanne. *Homophobia: A Weapon of Sexism*. Inverness, CA: Chardon Press, 1988.

Plumpp, Sterling. *Black Rituals*. Chicago: Third World Press, 1991.

Purvis, Sally B. *The Power of the Cross: Foundations for a Christian Feminist Ethic of Community*. Nashville: Abingdon Press, 1993.

Rasmussen, Larry L. *Moral Fragments & Moral Community: A Proposal for Church in Society*. Minneapolis: Fortress Press, 1993.

Richardson, Willie. "Evangelizing Black Males: Critical Issues and How-Tos." In *The Black Family: Past, Present, & Future*, ed. Lee N. June. Grand Rapids, MI: Zondervan Publishing, 1991.

Riggs, Marcia Y. *Awake, Arise & Act: A Womanist Call for Black Liberation*. Cleveland: Pilgrim Press, 1994.

_____. "The Logic of Interstructured Oppression: A Black Womanist Perspective." In *Redefining Sexual Ethics: A Sourcebook of Essays, Stories, and Poems,* ed. SusanE. Davies and Eleanor H. Haney. Cleveland: Pilgrim Press, 1991.

Roberts, J. Deotis. *Roots of a Black Future: Family and Church.* Philadelphia: Westminster Press, 1980.

Roberts, Samuel K. *African American Christian Ethics.* Cleveland: Pilgrim Press, 2001.

Sanders, Cheryl J., editor. *Living the Intersection: Womanism and Afrocentrism in Theology.* Minneapolis: Fortress Press, 1995.

_____. *Empowerment Ethics for a Liberated People.* Minneapolis: Fortress Press, 1995.

Smith, Althea, and Abigail J. Stewart, "Approaches to Studying Racism and Sexism in Black Women's Lives." *Journal of Social Issues.* 39/3 (1983).

Some, Malidoma Patrice. *Ritual: Power, Healing, and Community.* New York: Penguin Books, 1993.

Spelman, Elizabeth V. "'Race' and the Labor of Identity." In *Racism and Philosophy,* ed. Susan E. Babbitt and Sue Campbell. Ithaca, NY: Cornell University Press, 1999.

Stewart, James B. "Neoconservative Attacks on Black Families and the Black Male: An Analysis and Critique." In *The American Black Male: His Present Status and His Future,* ed. Richard G. Majors and Jacob U. Gordon. Chicago: Nelson-Hall Publishers, 1994.

Strong, Bryan, Christine DeVault, and Barbara Werner Sayad. *Core Concepts in Human Sexuality.* Mountain View, CA: Mayfield Publishing Company, 1996.

Taves, Ann. "Sexuality in American Religious History." In *Retelling U.S. Religious History,* ed. Thomas A. Tweed. Berkeley: University of California Press, 1997.

Taylor, Ronald L. "Black Males and Social Policy: Breaking the Cycle of Disadvantage." In *The American Black Male: His*

Present Status and His Future, ed. Richard G. Majors and Jacob U. Gordon. Chicago: Nelson-Hall Publishers, 1994.

Tinney, James S. "The Religious Experience of Black Men." In *Black Men,* ed. Lawrence E. Gary. Newbury Park, NJ: Sage Publications, 1981.

Townes, Emilie M. *In a Blaze of Glory: Womanist Spirituality as Social Witness.* Nashville: Abingdon Press, 1994.

Trull, Joe E., and James E. Carter. *Ministerial Ethics: Being a Good Minister in a Not-So-Good World.* Nashville: Broadman & Holman, 1993.

Turner, Victor. *The Ritual Process: Structure and Anti-Structure.* Ithaca, NY: Cornell University Press, 1969.

Vanzant, Iyanla. *The Spirit of a Man: A Vision of Transformation for Black Men and the Women Who Love Them.* San Francisco: HarperSan Francisco, 1996.

Walker, Theodore. *Empower the People: Social Ethics for the African-American Church.* Maryknoll, NY: Orbis Books, 1991.

Wallace, Michelle. *Black Macho and the Myth of the Super-woman.* New York: New Dial Press, 1979.

West, Candace, and Don H. Zimmerman. "Doing Gender." In *The Social Construction of Gender,* ed. Judith Lorber and Susan A. Farrell. Newbury Park, CA: SagePublications, 1991.

West, Cornel. *Race Matters.* Boston, MA: Beacon Press, 1993.
———. "On the Future of the Black Church." In *Prophetic Reflections: Notes on Race and Power in America.* Monroe, ME: Common Courage Press, 1993.

West, Traci C. "Spirit-Colonizing Violations: Racism, Sexual Violence, and Black American Women." In *Remembering Conquest: Feminist/Womanist Perspectives on Religion, Colonization, and Sexual Violence,* ed. Nantawan Boonprasat Lewis and Marie M. Fortune. Binghamton, NY: Haworth Pastoral Press, 1999.

White, Gayle. "Keeping Vigil: How Various Faiths Protect the Innocent in Their Flocks." *The Atlanta Journal-Constitution*. 14 September 2002.

Williams, Delores S. *Sisters in the Wilderness: The Challenge of Womanist God-Talk*. Maryknoll, NY: Orbis Books, 1993.

Williams, Linda Faye. "Power and Gender: A Glass Ceiling Limits the Role of Black Women in the Civil Rights Community." *Emerge*, December/January 1995.

Williamson, Marianne. *Illuminata: Thoughts, Prayers, Rites of Passage*. New York: Random House, 1994.

Wimberly, Edward P. "The Men's Movement and Pastoral Care of African American Men." In *The Care of Men*, ed. Christie Cozad Neuger and James Newton Poling. Nashville: Abingdon Press, 1997.

Wind, James P., Russell Burck, Paul F. Camenisch, and Dennis P. McCann, eds. *Clergy Ethics In a Changing Society: Mapping the Terrain*. Louisville: Westminster John Knox Press, 1991.

Wood, Frances E. "'Take My Yoke Upon You': The Role of the Church in the Oppression of African American Women." In *A Troubling in My Soul: Womanist Perspective on Evil & Suffering*, ed. Emilie M. Townes. Maryknoll, NY: Orbis Books, 1993.

Wyatt, Gail Elizabeth. *Stolen Women: Reclaiming Our Sexuality, Taking Back Our Lives*. New York: John Wiley & Sons, 1997.

INDEX

Abraham, 109
absolute control, 36
accountability, 19, 61, 98, 101
Acts, 93–94, 96–97, 98, 108–9, 110
adaptation, psychological, 45–46, 51–52, 53, 99
affirmative action, 57
African American church: black church transformation into, 86–87; as case study, 11–12; as community, 19–20; definitions, 17–20; functions of, 19–20; as site of sexual-gender oppression, 76–89; as supportive institution, 19, 20. *See also* black church; church; Negro church
African Methodist Episcopal (AME) Church, 10, 128
African Methodist Episcopal Zion (AMEZ) Church, 95–96, 128
African women, forced immigration of, 44–45
agency, 20–21, 47, 52, 76; moral agency, 18, 22, 98, 101–2
Allen, Robert L., 131
ambivalent American sexism, 81–83
American Black Male, The (Franklin), 48–49
American masculinity, 48–49
Ananias, 94, 110, 112–13
Anderson, Herbert, 136

Anderson, Victor, 134
anointed by the Spirit, 108–9
apostles, 93–94, 109
asymmetrical power, 87
Aunt Jemima, 40, 43, 60
authentic community, 116
authority: of clergy, 118; male authority in home and workplace, 41; women's authority in church, 83

Babbitt, Susan E., 131
Baptists, 81–82, 128
Barnabas, 93–94
Barton, Ronald G., 125
bearing good fruit, 109
behavior, sexualized, 86–87, 135
behavioral limits, 27
Bible, 123–24
biblical feminism, 81
biblical standards *vs.* cultural standards, 27
Bigger Thomas, 40, 43, 49
bishops, female, 10, 68–71
black church, 67; justice as core value, 86, 89; Negro church transformation into, 77–79; sexist ideology in, 81–82; as surrogate world, 80; transformation into African American church, 86–87. *See also* African American church; church
Black Church Since Frazier, The (Lincoln), 77–78

black family. *See* family
black liberation, 61–62, 78
black masculinities: conforming, 51, 52; innovative, 51, 52; mainstream society-controlled, 49, 50, 52; male peer group-controlled, 50, 52; negotiated from positions of powerlessness, 51; primary group-controlled, 49–50; rebellious, 52; retreatist, 51–52; ritualistic, 51; typologies of, 48–52
black men: as head of household, 38; as inferior, 39; internalization of sexual-gender myths, 48–50; male authority in home and workplace, 41; moral postures, 101; public leadership, 49; recognition as men, 48–49; sexism of, 43–44; slaves defined as subhuman non-men, 51; social construction of sex role, 51–52; socialization process for, 49–50; social myths, 39–40; subordination of, 40
Black Power, 78
black women: as backbone of the church, 87; bishops, 10, 68–71; as deficient/deviant from male-biased norm, 24, 25; independent African womanhood, 81; internalization of sexual-gender myths, 44–47; moral postures, 101; ordination of, 71, 82–83, 84, 88; as preachers, 82; slavery and, 44–46; social myths, 39–40;

stereotypes, 46–47; subordination of, 40, 42; virtues of, 38
blame, 43–44, 99, 106
Brawley, Robert L., 137
breeders, 45
Brittan, Arthur, 129
Broughton, Virginia, 133
Burck, Russell, 135
Burroughs, Nannie Helen, 133

call to ministry, 82, 88, 107
Camenisch, Paul F., 135
Campbell, Sue, 131
capitalism: racist-capitalist-patriarchal oppression, 38–39; racist-patriarchal-capitalist objectification, 99; racist-sexist-capitalist oppression, 54; white racist-sexist-capitalism, 44; white racist-sexist-capitalist patriarchal norms, 54
Carter, Stephen L., 102–3, 134, 135
Catholic natural law approach to sexuality, 25
challenging expectations, 109
character, 20–21, 47, 52; agency of the church and, 76; passing of character, 95–96; values and, 20, 21
children of God, 109
Chrisman, Robert, 131
Christian ethical reflection, 11–12
Christian ethics, 24–27, 122
Christian Methodist Episcopal (CME) Church, 128
Christian postmodern sexual ethic, 25
Christian sexual ethic, 122

church: birth of, 109–10; as community of the Spirit, 110; economy of, 97; ethics of common good, 107–8; as human community, 88–89, 105–6; as social institution, 88–89, 105–6; squelching the Spirit, 110; white church, 79. *See also* African American church; black church; Negro church
church doctrine, 21
church law, 75, 88
church mothers, 81
Church of God in Christ (COGIC), 128
church polity, 21, 88
circumcision, female, 130
civil rights movement, 41–42, 60, 77–78, 79
clergy: authority of, 118; laity relationships, 28–29, 88, 107–13; male clergy peer group, 84–85; role morality of, 28–29, 103, 105–6
clergy ethics, 11, 103–7; defined, 28–29; guidelines for, 124–26; power and, 103–6
codes of conduct, 28–29, 103, 121
codes of ethics, 135
common good, 107–8
communal ethics, 100–101
communal ethos of responsibility, 98
communal issues, 53
community: African American church as, 19–20; authentic community, 116; of belief and action, 20; human community, 19, 20, 88–89, 105–6; of interpretation, 19; of language, 19; of memory and understanding, 19; natural community, 19; political community, 19; of the Spirit, 110
competition, 65–66
complicity, 18, 53, 97–98, 106
conduct codes, 28–29, 103, 121
Cone, James H., 66, 132
confession of sin, 112
conflict: roots of black gender conflict, 36–37; traditions of, 81
conflict model of society, 19
conforming black masculinity, 51, 52
conservatism, 58, 60
control: absolute control, 36; black masculinities and, 50–52; justice *vs.* control of women, 87–88, 102; of women, as core value of patriarchal privilege, 86, 89
countersocialization, 99–103
Court of Appeal (Hill-Thomas case), 58
covenant to Abraham, 109
covert practices of oppression, 105
criticism, cultural and religious, 134
cultural criticism, 134
cultural practices, 44–45
cultural standards *vs.* biblical standards, 27

desire, structure of, 24, 83, 84–85

determinative institutions, 19
dignity, 46
discernment, 102–3
disciples, 93–94, 109
dissonance with the traditional, 115–16
division of labor, 24
Dodson, Jualynne E., 127
Douglas, Kelly Brown, 125
Douglass, Frederick, 49
Driver, Tom F., 136
dual-sex politics, 81
DuBois, W.E.B., 49
Dyson, Michael Eric, 132

ecclesial practices, 11
economic justice, 97
economic pressures, 37–39
economy of the church, 97
Ellison, Marvin, 125
emancipation, 37
enemies, loving, 109
ethics: Christian ethical reflection, 11–12; Christian ethics, 24–27, 122; of church's common good, 107–8; codes of, 135; communal ethics, 100–101; from Luke-Acts perspective, 109; ministerial ethics, 11, 28–29, 107–13; sexual ethics, 27, 122, 135; sexual-gender ethics, 9–10, 11, 21–28, 98–103; theological ethical framework, 108–11. *See also* clergy ethics
ethos: communal ethos of responsibility, 98; normative patriarchal institutional ethos, 86–87
eucharist, 112; ritual revision of, 113–16

expectations: challenging, 109; role expectations, 99–100
experience, 26
exploitation, 43–44

family: familial structures, 41; fragmented African familyhood, 81; as matriarchal, 41; slavery and, 45; West African familial organization, 81
Farrell, Susan A., 127
fatherhood roles, 53
female bishops, 10, 68–71
female circumcision, 131
female ministers, 71, 82–83, 84
female ordination, 71, 82–83, 84, 88
Fewell, Danna Nolan, 123
1 Corinthians, 67
1 Peter, 67
Foley, Edward, 136
forgiveness of sin, 112
formal practices, 21, 111
Fortune, Marie, 125
fragmented African familyhood, 81
Franklin, Clyde W., II, 48–52, 131–32
Franklin, Donna L., 31–32, 36–37, 129, 130
Frazier, E. Franklin, 77, 132
Free African Society of 1787, 128
Freedman's Bureau, 37–38
freed slaves, 37–38
Freire, Paulo, 31
Fulkerson, Mary McClintock, 135

gender: social construction of, 39; socioculturally constructed differences in, 24
gender conflict, 36–37

gender social groups, 22–23, 39–40, 53, 60–62
Giddings, Paula, 131
Gilkes, Cheryl Townsend, 80–82, 134
God, children of, 109
God's power, 108–9, 110, 111
God's reign, 110
God's Spirit. *See* Spirit
Gonzalez, Justo L., 136
Gordon, Jacob U., 130, 131
Gospel of Luke, 108–9
group membership, 45
groups: intragroup dynamics, 18; peer groups, 49–50, 52, 84–85; primary group, 49–50; social groups, 22–23, 39–40, 53, 60–62
group solidarity, 45
Gudorf, Christine E., 25, 125, 129
Gunn, Davis M., 123
Gustafson, James M., 128

Hahn, Celia Allison, 136
Hauerwas, Stanley, 135
head of household, 38
heterosexual patriarchal privilege, 104, 105–6
hierarchical relationships, as power relationships, 40
hierarchical sexual-gender relations, practices of, 110
hierarchy of needs, based on femaleness and maleness, 66
Hill, Anita, 54–62
Hill-Collins, Patricia, 127, 130
Holy Spirit. *See* Spirit
homosexuality, 75, 85, 88, 104, 106–7, 116
hooks, bell, 41–42, 60, 130

house slaves, 45
human community, 19, 20, 88–89, 105–6

ideals, 20, 21, 28
imbalance of power, 86–87, 103, 104–5
independent African womanhood, 81
inferiority, 39
informal practices, 21, 111
innovative black masculinity, 51, 52
institutional ethos, 86–87
institutions: determinative, 19; social, 88–89, 105–6; supportive, 19, 20
integrity, 86, 97, 102
internal dimension of oppression, 18
internalization: of racist-patriarchal-capitalist objectification, 99; of sexual-gender myths, by men, 48–50; of sexual-gender myths, by women, 44–47
intragroup dynamics, 18

Jack Johnson, 40, 43, 49, 60
Jackson, Jacquelyne Johnson, 132
Jackson, Jesse, 49
Janeway, Elizabeth, 129
Jesus, 108–10, 112
Jezebel, 40, 43, 60
Johnson, Lyndon B., 41
Jung, Patricia Beattie, 123
justice: as core value of black church, 86, 89; economic justice, 97; sexual-gender injustice, 88, 104–5; *vs.*

control of women, 87–88,
102. *See also* sexual-gender
justice

King, Martin Luther, Jr., 49,
59, 78

laity-clergy relationships,
28–29, 88, 107–13
leadership, 49, 83
Lebacqz, Karen, 125, 135, 136
lethal socialization triangle, 50
liberation: black liberation,
61–62, 78; women's liberation, 66
liberation Christian ethical reflection, 12
Lincoln, C. Eric, 77–79, 128,
133
Lorber, Judith, 127
loving one's enemies, 109
Lowery, Rev. Joseph E., 132
Luke, Gospel of, 108–9
lynching, 57, 58–59, 61

mainstream society-controlled
masculinity, 49, 50, 52
Majors, Richard G., 130, 131
male authority in home and
workplace, 41
male-biased norm, deficient/
deviant from, 24, 25
male clergy peer group, 84–85
male peer group-controlled
masculinity, 50, 52
male power, 23, 24
Mamiya, Lawrence H., 128
Mammy, 40, 46, 131
manhood, 39, 40, 42, 54, 60
Marable, Manning, 32, 129
marriage, 45

Martin, Clarice, 123
masculinity: American masculinity, 48–49; construction
of, 23; typologies of, 48–50,
51–52
Maynard, Mary, 129
McCann, Dennis P., 135
meaning structure, 100–101
media images, 40, 50
men. *See* black men; white men
Methodists, 10, 95–96, 128;
black denominations,
81–82; quadrilateral sources
for Christian ethics, 26
Meyers, William H., 134
militant patriarchal consciousness, 79
ministerial ethics, 11, 28–29,
107–13
ministers, female, 71, 82–83,
84
ministry, call to, 82, 88, 107
modesty and privacy, 45
Montgomery Bus Boycott, 78
moral agency, 18, 22, 98,
101–2
moral beings, 100
moral corruption, 86, 89, 102
moral education, 100–103
moral imagination, 95, 122
morality, 11–12; governing oppressive relations, 98–99;
role morality, 28–29, 53, 95,
103; role morality of clergy,
28–29, 103, 105–6; of sexual-gender injustice, 105; of
sexual-gender justice, 105–6;
sexual-gender morality, 100,
102–3, 104, 124–26; sexual-
gender role morality, 53,
100; social morality, 19

moral life, 18, 20–21, 87–88, 96–98, 103
moral postures, 101–2
moral vision, 95, 96–98, 108
Morrison, Toni, 60–61, 132
motherhood roles, 53, 81
Moynihan, Daniel, 41
Moynihan Report, 41
mutual service, 100, 110
myth. *See* sexual-gender social mythology; social mythology

narrative, 113
National Baptist Convention, U.S.A., Incorporated (NBC), 128
National Baptist Convention of American, Unincorporated (NBCA), 128
"nation within a nation" metaphor, 77
natural community, 19
natural law approach to sexuality, 25
Negro child/savage, 39
Negro church: as nation within a nation, 77; transformation into black church, 77–79. *See also* African American church; black church; church
Negro Church in America, The (Frazier), 77
Neuger, Christie Cozad, 129
normative patriarchal institutional ethos, 86–87
norms: male-biased, 24, 25; patriarchal, 54, 86–87; sexual, 27; sociocultural and socioethical, 41

objectification, 42–44, 53, 60, 62, 99
Office of Policy Planning and Research, 41
Opportunities for Industrialization Centers, 78
oppression, 66; covert/overt practices of, 105; definition, 22–23; internal dimension of, 18; morality governing oppressive relations, 98–99; practices of, 105–6; racist-capitalist-patriarchal oppression, 38–39; racist-sexist-capitalist oppression, 54; sexual-gender injustice as, 104–5; white racist oppression, 18. *See also* sexual-gender oppression
Orr, Judith L., 129
overt practices of oppression, 105

Paris, Peter J., 133
partnership, 106, 110
passing of character, 95–96
patriarchal privilege, 80, 101–2; control of women as core value of, 86, 89; heterosexual, 104, 105–6
patriarchy, 67; militant patriarchal consciousness, 79; normative patriarchal institutional ethos, 86–87; organized resistance to, 81; racist-capitalist-patriarchal oppression, 38–39; racist-patriarchal-capitalist objectification, 99; racist-sexist-capitalist norms, 54; sexist ideology from white tradi-

tions, 81–82; slave-master system, 48–49
Pauline epistles, 82
Pauline project of communal ethics, 100–101
peer groups: male clergy peer group, 84–85; male peer group-controlled masculinity, 50, 52; masculinities and socialization, 49–50
Pentecost, 109–10
personal fulfillment, 53
personality stereotypes, 40–43, 46–47
personhood, 82–83
pluralism, 17–18
policy, 40, 41
Poling, James Newton, 129
political community, 19
political conservatism, 58, 60
politics, dual-sex, 81
"Politics of 'Silence,' The" (Gilkes), 80–81
polity, 21, 88
postmodern sexual ethics, 25
power: abuse of clerical power, 99; clergy ethics and, 103–6; as commodity, 104–5; definition, 23; of God, 108–9, 110, 111; imbalance of, 86–87, 103, 104–5; male power, 23, 24; practice-based theory of power and gender, 23–24; practices of, 104; as practices of sexual-gender justice, 108; relational power, 105–6, 108, 110; sexual-gender injustice and, 104–5; social mythology and, 28; structure of, 24, 83–84; of white men, 39–40

powerlessness, 36, 51
power of the cross, 100–101, 110, 111
power of the Spirit, 111, 112
power relationships: asymmetrical, 87; hierarchical relationships as, 40
practice-based theory of power and gender, 23–24
practice of eucharist, 112
practices: cultural practices, 44–45; of dialogue, 106–7; ecclesial practices, 11; features of, 20–21; formal practices, 21, 111; fostering sexual-gender justice, 111–12; of hierarchical sexual-gender relations, 110; informal practices, 21, 111; of oppression, 105–6; of power, 104; practice-based theory of power and gender, 23–24; of relational power, 110; of resocialization, 111; of sexual-gender justice, 108; of sexual-gender oppression, 88–89; subverting, 109; taboo sexual practices, 47
preachers, women, 82
preaching style, 82
pregnancy, 82
primary group-controlled masculinity, 49–50
privacy and modesty, 45
privilege, 110. *See also* patriarchal privilege
Progressive National Baptist Conventions (PNBC), 128
psychological adaptation, 45–46, 51–52, 53, 99

public leadership, 49
public perception, 41
public policy, 40, 41
public witness, 96
Purvis, Sally, 135

Race-ing Justice, En-gendering Power, 58
racial sexual-gender social groups, 60–62
racial sexual-gender social mythology, 39–40
racism, 18, 41, 57, 59
racist-capitalist-patriarchal oppression, 38–39
racist oppression, white, 18
racist-patriarchal-capitalist objectification, 99
racist-sexist-capitalism, white, 44
racist-sexist-capitalist norms, 54
racist-sexist-capitalist oppression, 54
rape, 45
Rasmussen, Larry L., 129
reactive relations, 53, 54
reason, 26
rebellious black masculinity, 52
reflection, 11–12
relational power, 105–6, 108, 110
relations: creative, 43; hierarchical, 110; morality governing oppressive relations, 98–99; reactive relations, 53, 54; sexual-gender relations, 54, 110
relationships: hierarchical, 40; laity-clergy, 28–29, 88, 107–13; power relationships, 40, 87

relationship structures, 23–24; desire, 24, 83–84; labor, 23–24, 83–84; power, 24
relativism, 125–26
religious criticism, 134
resocialization, 100–102, 111
responsibility, 19, 98
resurrection of Jesus, 109–10
retreatist black masculinity, 51–52
rites of passage, 36, 44–45
ritual, 111–12; of the eucharist, 113–16
ritualistic black masculinity, 51
role expectations, 99–100
role morality: of clergy, 28–29, 103, 105–6; sexual-gender, 53, 100
roles: fatherhood roles, 53; leadership roles, 83; motherhood roles, 53, 81; from sexual-gender morality, 100; sexual-gender roles, 36, 99, 100; slavery and women's roles, 45; social construction of, 51–52; socialization and, 42
"Roles of Church and Community, The" (Gilkes), 80–81
roots of black gender conflict, 36–37

sacraments, 21, 112, 113–16
Sambo, 40
Sands, Kathleen M., 129
Sapphira, 94, 110, 112–13
Sapphire, 40, 43
scenarios, 12–13, 33–35, 47–48, 52, 68–75; analysis of, 83–88
scripts, 87, 89, 100
scripture, 26

secrecy, 46
selective patronage, 78
self-actualization, 62, 88, 99
self-definition, 78
self-determination, 49, 78
Senate confirmation process, 54–62
sex: meaning of, 44–45; *vs.* gender, 24
sexism: ambivalent American sexism, 81–83; of black men, 43–44; male-based norm and, 25; racist-sexist-capitalist oppression, 54; white racist-sexist-capitalism, 44; white racist-sexist-capitalist patriarchal norms, 54
sexist ideology, 81–82
sexual abuse, 47
sexual contact: between family members, during slavery, 45; unethical, 86–87
sexual ethics, 27, 135; Christian, 11–12, 25, 122; postmodern, 25
sexual-gender countersocialization, 101–2, 103
sexual-gender ethics, 9–10, 11, 21–28, 98–103
sexual-gender identity, 22
sexual-gender injustice: based in power as a commodity, 104–5; morality of, 105; as oppression, 104–5; perpetuating, 88; power and, 104
sexual-gender justice, 62, 103; moral corruption and, 86; morality of, 105–6; power as practices of, 108; practices fostering, 111–12; theological ethical framework for, 108–11

sexual-gender morality: guidelines for, 124–26; heterosexual male standards of, 104; roles from, 100; social construction of, 102–3; values and, 100
sexual-gender oppression: African American church as site of, 76–89; complicity with, 53; perpetuating within African American community, 54–62; practices of, 88–89; support of, 20; values and, 88–89
sexual-gender relations, 54, 110
sexual-gender role morality, 53, 100
sexual-gender roles, 36, 99, 100
sexual-gender scripts, 87, 89, 100
sexual-gender self-actualization, 62
sexual-gender social groups, 39–40, 53, 60–62
sexual-gender socialization, 99–101
sexual-gender social mythology: black men and women, 39–40; of gender social groups, 39–40; internalization of, 43–50; Moynihan Report as example, 41; racial, 39–40; sexual-gender socialization and, 99–100
sexual harassment, 10, 43–44, 54–56, 60
sexual identity, 22, 75, 85, 88
sexuality: of black women preachers, 82; natural law approach to, 25; tensions and, 117

sexualized behavior, 86–87, 134
sexual misconduct, 88
sexual norms, 27
sexual practices, taboo, 47
shadow work, social reproductive, 54, 61
sharecropping, 37–38
She-Devil, 46, 131
silence, 46, 86, 112
sin, confession and forgiveness of, 112
sins of omission and commission, 112
slavery, 18, 36, 44–46; black men as subhuman non-men, 51; black women and, 44–46; family and, 45; freed slaves, 37–38; lynching, 57, 58–59, 61; patriarchal slavemaster system, 48–49
Smith, Ralph E., 123
social construction: of black male sex role, 51–52; of gender, 39; of manhood and womanhood, 40; of roles, 51–52; of sexual-gender morality, 102–3; social mythology and, 27–28
social construction gender theory, 24–27, 59–60, 122
social groups, 22–23, 39–40, 53, 60–62
socialization: of black men, 49–50; countersocialization, 99–103; lethal socialization triangle, 50; roles and, 42, 87; sexual-gender, 99–101; sexual-gender scripts and, 87, 89; values and, 87
social morality, 19

social mythology, 124; power and, 28; social construction of gender and, 27–28. *See also* sexual-gender social mythology
social reproductive shadow work, 54, 61
Sojourner Truth, 133
Some, Malidoma Patrice, 136
Southern Christian Leadership Conference, 59, 78
Speaks, Joan C., 12–13
Spelman, Elizabeth V., 132
Spirit, 109–10, 112; anointed by, 108–9; community of, 110; power of, 111, 112; squelching, 110
standing in the gap, 74
stereotypes, 40–43, 46–47
Stewart, Maria, 133
Stolen Women (Wyatt), 44
storytelling, 112, 113
structure: family structures, 41; meaning structure, 100–101; power of, 24, 83–84; of relationships, 23–24, 83–84
Student Nonviolent Coordinating Committee, 78
subordination: of black men, 40; of black women, 40, 42, 80, 87; of white women, 40
Sullivan, Leon, 78
supportive institution, 19, 20
supportive presence, 116
symbol system, 100–101

taboo sexual practices, 47
tension, 117, 118
theological ethical framework, 108–11
Thomas, Clarence, 54–62

Townes, Emilie M., 66, 132
tradition: of biblical feminism, 81; of conflict, 81; dissonance with the traditional, 115–16; sexist ideology from white traditions, 81–82; source of Christian ethics, 26
transformation, 111
Truth, Sojourner, 133
Turner, Henry McNeal, 49
typology of black masculinities, 48–50, 51–52

Uncle Tom, 40, 43, 49, 60
union service, 75, 85
unity, 100, 110

values: character and, 20, 21; control of women as, 86, 89; inconsistency of, 86, 87–88, 89, 102; justice as, 86, 89; sexual-gender morality and, 100; sexual-gender oppression and, 88–89; socialization and, 87
Vanfossen, Beth E., 128
virtues, 20, 21, 38, 100

Walker, Alice, 127
Wallace, Michelle, 130
Washington, Booker T., 49
Welfare Queen, 40
West, Candace, 127
West, Cornel, 42–43, 60, 130
West African familial organization, 81

What's Love Got To Do with It? (Franklin), 36
white church, 79
white men, 39–40
white racism, 18, 59
white racist oppression, 18
white racist-sexist-capitalism, 44
white racist-sexist-capitalist patriarchal norms, 54
white women, 39–40
Williams, Linda Faye, 67, 132
Williamson, Marianne, 136
Wind, James P., 135
womanhood, 38–39, 40, 54
womanist, 127
womanist assessment, 79–89
womanist Christian ethical reflection, 11–12
women: authority in the church, 83; leadership roles in the church, 83; ministers, 71, 82–83, 84; organizations within the church, 81
Women's Day, 81, 133
women's liberation, 66
women's work, 68, 84
Workhorse, 46, 131
Wyatt, Gail Elizabeth, 44, 46–47, 130
Wynn, Prathia Hall, 134

Young, Andrew, 49
Young, Iris Marion, 129

Zimmerman, Don H., 127